IF IT'S NOT
ONE THING
IT'S A

IF IT'S NOT
ONE THING
IT'S A
Mother

HOW FAITH,
HEALTH, AND
OLD SCHOOL
PARENTING
HAVE SHAPED
MY LIFE

Sabrina
—Ciceri—

Contents

Introduction

I WAS HIDING IN A CAR. Not my car, because she would have recognized it, but someone else's car. I'd paid a guy to follow my mom because she was wrecking her life but wouldn't admit it. I knew though because I had hacked her Facebook account. That's when I saw that my mom was cheating on the first good guy she'd married in a long time with some weirdo artist who was on disability and was my age. He said she was his muse, his angel, and the sex talk was sickening.

She denied it, so I needed pictures to show what was going on. Well, I got 'em. She was getting into his car, kissing him. Triumph! I knew it! I could finally help her. I then showed them to my stepdad, who she'd said was okay with her having a fling on the side. But was he? Now she said she was in love with the new man; that he was her soulmate. What in the world is wrong with her? How many dozens, yes DOZENS of times had I heard that? I ask again, what in the world is wrong with her?

But then...

What in the world is wrong with me?

Why do I keep doing this? Since the time when I was a teenager and found out my mom had run off with my boyfriend, also a teenager, I have struggled mightily to understand my mother. I have also worked tirelessly to get my mom back, to recapture the friendship we had before I knew how crazy she was. For most of my adult life, I have been trying to change my mom. She is now sixty-nine years old, and I'm starting to think that when it comes to men and constantly needing love from a new one, she can't be changed.

What's worse is that I'm starting to realize that I might be the one who needs to change.

This is a book about my mother. I don't expect you to have a mother as crazy as mine, but I do know that you have or had a mother. I can promise you that there are some good qualities about you that you can trace back to her. Like me, you have some good things that your mom put there, but you also have some hurt, some crazy, some habits, and some thought patterns that are there. You just may not know it.

I can also promise you that your life is being impacted by what you've inherited from her. You are doing things because of the way you were raised by your mom. If you are a mother, then you are dramatically impacted by your own mother. You may be doing things just like she did, or you may be striving to do the opposite, because God forbid that you are *anything* like her! But that is still bondage.

I want to share some of my own journey with my mother and see if I can help you and me both get to a place of understanding and wisdom. There are things I've learned, and there are things I'm still trying to learn. Some things I will teach you, and maybe we can learn some other things together by the time we get to the last page.

I come to you now as a woman who loves being a mother. In fact, it is the most important aspect of my identity. This is a book about mothers, for mothers, by a mother. If you are not a mother, you can still read it and I hope you find it interesting and helpful, but the title says it all.

I'll tell you right now that Jesus is the source of everything good about my life, so I will unapologetically point to him throughout this book. I shudder to think where I would be without him. I have a lot of stories to tell, so I hope you are ready. I hope you are prepared to face your own stories, because when you do, you can heal. Once you heal, you can really start living.

If you have things in your life that are holding you back from a joyful, abundant existence, then let me suggest, *if it's not one thing, it's a mother!*

Chapter 1

My Ideal Childhood—
If Only it Could Have Lasted

"When you give joy to other people,
you get more joy in return"
–Eleanor Roosevelt

I LOVED BEING A LITTLE GIRL. I loved being a little mama to my dolls, animals, and every kid I knew who was younger than me. Why wouldn't I want to be a mom? I had the greatest mom in the world. She was absolutely stunning, kind, warm, and affectionate, and she spent lots of time with me, her only child.

I had a handsome, wise, hardworking, and perfect dad, too. He was always teaching me things, disciplining me with a gentle and consistent hand, and he was in love with my mom.

The three of us were thick as thieves and enjoyed a perfect existence. What more could a little girl want?

My dad worked a lot, but when he wasn't working, he played with me and did things around the house. My dad was always busy and that made him happy. His nicknames for me were Sabby, Saychmo, and every other cute little name he could think of. I helped my dad build a deck, and somehow he found time to "ride me in the wheelbarrow" and take me on bike rides to watch him play basketball, or to go swimming at the city pool where he'd throw me around all day long.

My beautiful mom would be there too, at the pool, sunbathing. She was not a "playing" mother, but a nurturer, cleaner, and cook. I was her little doll, and she took very good care of me and stood up for me when necessary. I can tell by looking at old photos that Mom was very much all about me in those days. My hair was always done in pigtails, and I wore the cute little halter sundresses and tube tops that were popular for little girls in the '70s. I even had cute little hippy bell bottoms.

Ask that little girl, and she will tell you that things were absolutely perfect. It was a perfect world and a perfect family filled with swimming, dancing, and piano lessons. I had a matching backpack and lunch box for school and always wore a new outfit on the first day of school.

At night, we'd always have something yummy like spaghetti with sauce that mom had been simmering on the stove all day. If she wasn't stirring sauce, she was cheerfully peeling potatoes, stringing green beans, or preparing any number of things from our full and abundant pantry. Plenty of the things she offered were the good unhealthy stuff; the best stuff at the time, like marshmallow cream, cheese puffs, double stuffed Oreos, real mayonnaise, and then at some point, the greatest invention of all time, ranch dressing! I remember the commercial for it vividly, "The original and best from Hidden Valley".

My goodness, I remember it all like heaven. Dairy Queen still used Texas toast for their hotdogs. If you went to McDonalds, Ronald still walked around hugging all the kids. My favorite? Long John Silvers! That was the only "seafood place" in small town West Virginia, but it was perfect. I still don't know what magic (evil magic) formula they use to make that batter. It's on my bucket list to figure out because there is nothing like it in any fine seafood restaurant in Key West! Their coleslaw is not too bad, either.

We lived in a coal mining town, and those miners ate tons of ground beef, meatloaf, and mashed potatoes. Why so much about food? Because food was a huge part of my childhood. Everything centered around food when I was growing up. Going to Mamaw's, I'd get homemade breakfast—biscuits, gravy, all of it from scratch. Then they'd clean up the kitchen and start making lunch. After lunch, they'd start making dinner.

Food was a constant, and we kids were expected to jump in and help. Even though I was an only child, I had cousins, and we all helped out by shucking corn, stringing beans, and peeling potatoes. I'm laughing now as I remember how much I hated those jobs, but it comes back to me as a fond memory. I remember all those days as better and better the older I get.

As ideal as my childhood was, I do remember my parents fighting. They were young and in love, but the passion they both had sometimes meant conflict. When they argued I would worry so much about mom, because she would cry, and I desperately wanted her to feel better. I probably did things to comfort her, and probably thought a lot about how to make her feel better.

For a long time, my dad worked the night shift. I loved it, because then I could sleep in the bed with Mom. I remember feeling so safe. The safety of being with your mom is a different kind than you feel with your dad. Your dad will protect you from monsters, and he will not let any bad guys come into the house. He will pick you up and hold you high if the waves are too strong, so the ocean doesn't knock you down.

The thing about a mom is that she will protect you from sadness. She will kiss your boo boos and make everything better on the inside. She'll wash your hair and lovingly make sure that the soap stays out of your eyes. Mom is the tenderness that every child needs. Mom doesn't need to teach you to be tough. That can be for dad. My mom was good for tenderness, and in that way, a wonderful mom.

My dad was twenty and my mom was seventeen when I was born. Though they got married because my mom was pregnant with me, they were very much in love. My dad was an incredibly hard worker and always made plenty of money, but he liked spending it too, and always managed to spend just a little more than he made. The only other person I know with a work ethic that comes close to that of my father is the man I married, and he was mentored by my father.

Mom always made sure to get me the things that I needed. She saw that my friends got to come over and play, maybe to make up for me having no brothers or sisters. It truly was a great childhood. I played with baby dolls and cooked for them in my burnt orange and olive green play kitchen (it was the '70s!). I played all day long, and sometimes I played teacher. Whatever the game was, it had something to do with me bossing people around and telling them what to do!

Everything was wonderful. Christmas, birthdays, any holiday with fireworks, it was all good. My parents hardly ever did anything without me. We were tight, a happy gang of three, and we grew up together. Then, when I was in the seventh grade, my mother ran off with my sixteen-year-old boyfriend.

Chapter 2

So Much for an Ideal Childhood–How it Fell to Pieces

"Don't let yesterday take too much of today."
–Will Rogers

I WAS THIRTEEN YEARS OLD, and my dad had a little pool hall he ran down on Main Street in our town. He didn't sell alcohol, but he sold candy and snacks. He was always trying to figure out some way to make money, and everybody in town hung out there. Our town was small, so I could walk everywhere from our house. After junior high school let out, I'd walk home, but sometimes I'd walk to the pool hall.

There was a boy, James, that hung out there and I thought he was really cute. He said he was sixteen, which was a little old for me, but he liked me, and anyway, I looked more like sixteen than thirteen. I wasn't allowed to date, but James had gotten to know my dad enough that my dad let him walk me home from the pool hall some days.

My dad's day job was as a postal carrier, and at night he worked in the pool hall until about 9:00. James would come to the house and hang out with Mom and me. We'd sit around outside chatting or walk around the neighborhood together. I took a big step and held hands with him sometimes.

Here's where it starts getting weird. In a small town like that, one of the few things to do is drive up and down the main drag, doing what, I don't know, but you'd see other people and honk the horn and wave. That's not the weird part. The weird part is that my mother liked to drive us up and down the drag like she was one of us teenagers, out having a good time. It got even weirder when she wanted to get some beer to drink and she even let me have a little bit, which I thought was gross.

I sound like a broken record, but things just kept getting weirder and I was too naive to see it. My parents drank maybe once or twice per year on holidays, but for some reason they had dry gin in the house. One evening when the three of us (my Mom, James, and I) were sitting around, my mom got out three little Cornell teacups, the white ones with the blue flowers your grandmother probably had, and the three of us sat at the table drinking gin. I, of course, became drunk as a skunk and had to be put to bed. As I drifted off to sleep, I could hear my mother and my boyfriend in the kitchen laughing and having a good time.

About a week later, when I got out of school, James was not there to meet me to walk home, which was the first time in a while he hadn't been there. I walked home alone, a little perplexed, and then became more perplexed when I arrived home and James was already there. "How odd," I remember thinking, but also, at thirteen, I didn't think any deeper than that, except that the door had been locked.

My mom said, "Oh, sorry," as she let me in.

Then, one fateful Friday, I got home from school and my dad was home. This was unusual. He said, "Hey, you know, your mom and I are having a little problem here. She says I work too much, and she's taking the weekend to go see Mamaw."

Mamaw, my maternal grandmother, lived about forty-five minutes away. My mom had never done that before, and since we only had one car, my dad and I were stranded. That's when I told my dad about the weird stuff that had been going on, how I came home and the door was locked, but James was there, and how I went to bed while they stayed up. My dad understood this better than I did. I also told him that it was such a coincidence that mom was out of town because James was also going out of town to see his family for a while. Dad could see what was going on.

Dad found an old blue Chevy Impala in the newspaper for $800 and he talked the guy into letting us have it for $400 now, $400 later, and even got him to deliver the car to us at the house. That car would overheat, so to keep it going, you had to run the heater, even in summer. This would move the heat from the engine into the cab. The car wouldn't overheat, but the passengers would!

Dad said we were going to surprise "mom an' them." We got there as dark was coming on. This was the town both my parents grew up in, so my dad was trying not to be seen. We parked way down the street in this car nobody knew. He put his arm around me and told me to keep my head down.

Nobody saw us as we came around on the road on the back side of Mawmaw's house. When we got to the front, there was my mother sitting on the porch with my boyfriend. James started to cry at the sight of my father, who, if I haven't said it already, is six foot three inches tall and weighed about 300 pounds at the time. James was a scared kid.

My dad was a kind man, and he said to James, "Listen, go on inside. Stay in the house. You're just a kid. You don't have to be afraid of me. I'm not gonna do anything to you."

James walked inside, relieved.

To my mom, Dad said, "What are you doing? This is crazy."

She just cried. After they talked a little bit, my dad and I got in the car and went back home, completely stupefied. The next day, my mother came back to the house and said that she was in love with James, that he was eighteen, not sixteen, and she was moving with him to North Carolina to live with his family.

I remember how I cried as she packed her bag. I was thirteen! We had had such a good life up to that point. I had no idea my parents had been struggling with their relationship. I loved my dad so much, and simply could not understand this alternative universe I had suddenly been plunged into by the craziness of my mom. I remember begging and pleading with her, "Why can't you stay for me?"

Do you know what she said? She said she had given me all of her life, and I had gotten to be a smarty pants thirteen-year-old, and didn't need her as much, and I didn't want to be hugged anymore. She was in love, she said. She was sorry that it hurt me, but she had to go.

And that was the end of my childhood. Mom left, and within two days my dad sold almost everything we had, put the rest in a U-Haul, and pulled it with that old Chevy Impala to South Carolina, running the heat the whole way. We rented an apartment down the street from my dad's brother, who owned a roofing business. My aunt Pat drove me to school and back every day, and my dad worked and made money. His main goal with that move was to get out of the town where he'd been humiliated. He wanted a fresh start.

In hindsight, I have a better understanding of how even the early years were not so perfect, but back then, I lamented what I felt I'd lost. How could my mom, my best friend, leave me like that? This was only the first of many, many times I'd have to ask that sad question. I still get the chance to ask it today at least once a year. So, was my mom going to marry this boy child? If you are thinking this is insane, you are right! I had no idea what to expect from then on in this alternate universe.

After about a month, my mom felt like she missed me terribly. I hadn't talked to her very much. We didn't have cell phones or pagers, you just had to be around the house when the phone rang. She asked me to come see her. As mad and hurt as I was, I missed her, too. My heart ached, but whether it was for my mom or for the character she'd played in my life, I didn't know, but I missed her more than she missed me and wanted to go see her. My dad agreed to drive me to North Carolina to leave me there for the weekend. They planned to meet halfway on Sunday so I could return to South Carolina. It was a six-hour drive.

He left me there on Friday, and after a brief tearful hello, she left me downstairs with James's family, while she stayed in the bedroom the whole evening, doing God knows what. Well, I do know some of it, because they had the kind of peephole you could see through, and I looked in there at one point and saw them laying together. Sitting there with his family all night, I started to wonder what I was doing there. They were nice enough, but I hadn't come to see them.

The next day, she took me to see a couple of his other family members, but then we quickly went back home, and she'd disappear again with him in their bedroom, leaving me to hang out with his brother and sister. She just wasn't into me at all, and it felt just terrible for me at thirteen. Again, I felt rejected.

By God's grace, my dad called to check on me Saturday. I got on the phone with him and just fell apart crying. "Daddy, it's horrible. I wish I didn't have to stay. Mom is spending no time with me…" I told him everything. "She's just pinned up in the bedroom with him, and I can't handle it. She doesn't want to be with me, and I wish I could go home."

My dad said, "Don't worry. I didn't leave. I got a motel room down the street because I was afraid that if something like this happened and you needed me, I would be too far away."

So, he came over within five minutes to get me. I had my bag packed and felt relieved to be leaving. When he pulled up and I went out to the car, my mom came running outside. "What are you doing? You're supposed to stay until tomorrow evening!"

Dad said, "Don't you speak to her! She came here to visit you and you aren't even spending time with her. You won't get her again!"

And we went back to South Carolina.

One month went by, and my mom wanted to come back to us.

For the first time of many, my Dad took her back. She said she didn't want to be in that relationship anymore. James had gotten mad at her and busted out her car windshield, but she was still living with his parents with no way to make money. She had taken a job at a gas station, but for my mom, the Prima Donna, that was quite a come down. She had been raised with money, being from one of the wealthier families in town. My Papaw was a boss in one of the coal mines, so she was used to having matching outfits, handbags, and everything she wanted. This was degrading for her, so she came home. Dad was happy to take her back. She was his weakness and would be for most of his life.

In an interesting side note, in my dad's loneliness, he'd actually begun to date another woman already. My mom, full of "righteous" rage, descended upon her house, cussed her out, and told her to keep her hands off her man. Straight from a trashy soap opera!

By then, the fairytale had ended and my bubble had burst. The real and fallen world full of brokenness had revealed itself to me. My mom was back, and I was happy, but she was crazy, and I knew it. I'd learn to dread whatever craziness hid around the next corner.

It was my relationship with Jesus that got me through this trying time, and many more times after that. He is without a doubt the real hero of my story. God and therapy have helped me a lot. I am a person who naturally looks for and sees the good in people. I don't think I'm naive, and I know I'm not stupid, but I'm also drawn to help those who are in the prison of their own hurts and their own horrible decisions. I think there should be consequences for people's behavior, but I have a lot of compassion for people in hard situations.

That said, the person I have the least patience with is my mother. I've always loved her, but I know I sometimes can't help but treat her poorly. Why? I think it is because I have never quite been able to set the right boundaries with her. When you don't set boundaries, you tend to resent people. When you resent people, there is no way to hide your feelings.

For me, the resentment tends to come in the form of harsh comments. I love my mom, but I can't help myself sometimes. Even when things are good, I'll make a scathing comment like, "You're doing good now, but wait until you find a man again."

My husband Joe says I'm too sharp with her, that I should be nice to her. I say, "Well, I'm on edge all the time, waiting for her to abandon me again."

If I need to go into a Hallmark store to find a card for her, I get stuck. I know she's done the best that she can, but something broken in her makes her seek out fulfillment in men. Even today at sixty-nine years old! If she were anybody else, I'd just feel sorry for them, but she's my mom, and her choices hurt! I think I stay so angry at her because I want her to do better. I want her to find God and figure out a healthy and true way to get herself fulfilled in a way no man on Earth could do. I feel like I'm mad at her all the time.

After we all got back home together, things seemed okay for a while, though they would be forever changed. Just as I began to process that my mother had run away with my boyfriend, she ran away with another guy. I'll talk later about my experiences as a mother to my children, but from thirteen on, I have felt like a mother to my mother, and that is a trip!

Reba McIntyre's song "Is There Life Out There" seems to be the theme song of my mother's life. *Is there life out there, so much I haven't done. Is there life out there beyond my family and my home?*

If I haven't said it already, my mother has always been drop-dead gorgeous. She looks a bit like a cross between Jane Seymour and Crystal Gayle. She has fiery green eyes, and usually, a sweet disposition. Even in childhood pictures I've seen of my mother, she looks adorable.

Her Drug of Choice

With those great looks and that adorable demeanor, she could easily hook a man, and this became her drug of choice, especially if she was drinking. Male attention was her fuel. It still is today. Even now, she has a husband who we all love, and she has another man on the side. By the time this book goes to be published, there will probably be another one. My stepdad is the sweetest man, and he takes good care of her, but one man is just not enough for my mother.

It is never a fling in her mind when she starts out. My mother falls in love hard and fast. Every guy she got with from James on, and there were many, she thought was her soulmate, and she needed to marry him.

I became an adult at thirteen, and the mom to both of my parents (oh, we'll talk more about my dad later). I was the responsible one, always trying to talk my mom off a cliff. She would run off with her new soul mate, then of course things would fall apart, and she'd come running back to my dad feeling awful and guilty. She'd run off to get married, and then, no, "Never mind, I don't want to live in poverty with this guy who, as it turns out, has some anger issues and drinks too much."

Dad, the Enabler

Every time Mom left, my dad thought he was done putting up with her. Then he'd start missing her, and when she ran back to him, he'd take her back—every time. His loyalty and commitment to her was crazy. I wish it was because he was a Christian and valued his marriage vows so highly, but no, he was just naive and had my mom on a pedestal. He loved and adored her. Men were her weakness, and she was his weakness.

I will say there was one good long stretch where they were together from the time I was about fifteen to when I was thirty. As far as I know, my mom behaved pretty well, and then, as though a bomb inside her went off, she started flirting and hanging out with guys. She left my dad again when she was nearly fifty.

When this cycle happens, it is brutal to watch. It is hard to watch someone you love make such a disaster of her life. It is even harder when it is the person who is supposed to be your example. But what made this beyond hard, what made it cause fractures in my own heart, was and is the fact that whenever mom goes off on one of her star-crossed romances, *she wants absolutely nothing to do with me or my family.* She has tunnel vision like a cat in heat.

I've been a Christian so long that I hardly remember what it was like not to have God in my life and the Holy Spirit in my heart. We all have a void in our hearts and seek ways to fill it. I've filled my void with God. For some, they might turn to food, for others, status, and still others, approval. For my mom, her void looks like the aching need to be catching a man. It is not enough that my dad was crazy for her. He was a workaholic and wasn't around enough to help fill that void. Filling her void means she needs the promise of a new romance. A sign that she's still got it. Even today, this is my sixty-nine-year-old mom's drug of choice, her idol, her god.

Gone Again

At age thirty, mom was off again, absent from my life. As much as I shouldn't have been surprised, it crushed me. I am close to my mom. We have been tightly bound since I was a little girl in love with her, and we had a closeness that bordered on unhealthy. I was her little best friend; her doll. My dad worked every night, so it was just us. My mom battled fear when he was gone and would have me sleep in their bed with her. There was no boundary there, and my attachment to her was beyond healthy.

I know that I was her best and only friend. In those days, when my dad's workaholism left her feeling empty, she poured all of her love into me. As a little girl, I loved and craved it. I didn't know that it wasn't about me. I couldn't understand that it was about her; that in some weird way she was doing with me what she would do with men later, filling an emotional hole. I just thought she loved me.

My first realization about her unhealthy view of relationships came the first time she ran off, the time with James, my boyfriend. How could that possibly happen? How could her love be a zero-sum equation? Most people are able to love their children in a special way that comes from an infinite reserve. God loves us like that.

> But Zion said, "I don't get it. God has left me.
> My Master has forgotten I even exist."
> "Can a mother forget the infant at her breast,
> walk away from the baby she bore?
> But even if mothers forget,
> I'd never forget you—never.
> —Isaiah 49:14-15 (MSG)

We all understand the unconditional love of a mother. I understand this love because I am a mother, not because I am a daughter. Thankfully, as a little child I believed that my mother loved me this way, but later, I could only see that her love for me had and still has a selfish and expedient quality. She loves me when it suits her. She loves affection, and her priority is men, but when there is no man, she will settle for me. Understanding that hurts. It's a wisdom that is painfully accepted.

Being put on an equal plane with my parents was not good for me. I needed to be their child, not their buddy, and certainly not their parent. They argued and put me in the middle of it. Money was usually the subject of the arguments, and they did nothing to shelter me from the stress of it. My father was an extremely hard worker, but, man, he loved to spend money. He liked nice things, and this made finances tight. I can remember going to the grocery store and mom writing a huge check, "Because if we were going to bounce a check, might as well make it worth it!"

That said, I never wanted for anything material, and still think of my childhood, at least up to age thirteen, as a good one. In the remaining chapters, I'll distill the wisdom I've gained from the search for healing from all this craziness.

Chapter 3

Sticks and Stones—The Power of Words to Kill and to Heal

"It is better to fail in originality than to succeed in imitation"
—Herman Melville

YOU KNOW THAT OLD SAYING, "Sticks and stones may break my bones, but words will never hurt me?"

Well, don't you believe it, because sticks and stones will just break your bones. Bones heal, but words can ruin you for life.

I am thankful that I can't think of very many instances where words used against me created life-long scars. The problem is that it doesn't take many words. One word, one sentence can lodge itself so deeply that you are affected by it forever. One lie, one harsh word, or one belittlement can infect all of your choices and behaviors, and some may never realize the damage that's been done.

In case you think it is only the words of childhood that scar, think again. Even today, I am vigilant about what words I let people say to me because I know words go deep. The most impactful negative words were those spoken from my mother, and the most vicious were those spoken to me as an adult.

She Said What?

One day I was crying about my mom's crazy behavior. I was exhausted and worried about her. I said, "You know, I have hurt ever since you first left Dad."

I told her that the burden of her being like one of my children was so much to handle. She started crying. I thought, "Wow, she finally sees that she's hurt me."

But then the words that came out of her mouth next blew me away. She said, "You know, if it hurt you, can you imagine how hard it was for me living through all that?"

My tears dried up with her unfathomable statement. Her response made me realize even more that my mom is extremely self-centered at her deepest core, *and there's nothing I can do about it.*

She is about herself first. I do think she loves me dearly in her way, but first, there's the preservation of Belinda (that's my mom's name). That's her number one thought, period, so she always manages to cast herself as the victim. In this case, the real damage was not the words she spoke, but the meaning behind the words. I heard them coming straight from the Devil. "Your pain is not important to me. I don't care that you felt abandoned by the one person on Earth who was called to nurture you. *You are not important.*"

Honestly, I feel demonized sometimes by the anger this causes in me. Words have power.

I wish that I could say that after all these years I am impervious to the power of negative words, but I'm not. If someone questions my integrity, it's terrible, because in actuality I work very hard to always do the right thing. I love God and seek to conduct my life and business in the most honest, fair, and generous way possible. But let one person, no matter how corrupt, say words that question my integrity, and I become insecure about it. I doubt myself and feel chastised, as though I had done something wrong. Words have great power. Use them wisely.

I have studied hard to master whatever subject was important at various stages of my life. I earned my nursing license. I learned about business. I learned about the law as I fought for my children. I learned God's Word so I could know him and please him. God has given me a sharp mind, but let one person call me dumb, and suddenly I feel less than.

I believe in myself. I believe what God says about me, that I have worth in his eyes. I believe I have been a successful person in all areas of my life. I believe I am the best me I can be. I work on myself, and I love to grow. I know I'm not perfect, but I know what I'm becoming.

Furthermore, I know God loves me, and therefore I love myself enough to steward my body and my life. But let one person tear me down, let my mother reject me with her words or actions, and my self-esteem goes into the toilet. Why? *Because words have power.*

The Good News

And there is good news here because *words have power*! This means I can use words to build up myself and others. Words are rebuilding me. Where does this process start? With the Word of God! Isn't it amazing that the Bible is called *the Word*. It's even more amazing and powerful that Jesus is called the Word. It is Jesus himself who can heal us from the terrible damage caused by the words of people and the lying words of Satan.

Chapter 4

I Said "I Do" to the Same Guy Three Times When it Should Have Been My Dad Marrying Him!

"It is better to fail in originality than to succeed in imitation."
–Herman Melville

I MET MY FIRST HUSBAND in my junior year in high school. He had come to our town for a year from New York with his parents. His dad was a schoolteacher, and he was on a sabbatical. Since his grandmother lived here and had an extra home where they stayed, he ended up spending three years in Florida.

We started dating, and at the end of my junior year I lost my virginity to him. In spite of the way my mother is, I was not raised to do that, so what I did was considered terrible by my parents, and in some ways by me.

My parents found out and my dad forced their family to leave town. His dad decided they would go back to New York.

He didn't want the drama because my dad was so upset. Steve had had sex a lot. He was just a year older than me, but since he was eighteen and I was only seventeen, my dad somehow got the Florida Department of Children and Families (DCF) involved and had him accused of statutory rape.

My parents were strict, but Steve was sneaky. He rode his bike over and snuck in my window. That's how we would get together because I was so closely watched. It's crazy to me now that I did that, but I did. Dad found out about it when he picked up the phone and heard us in a conversation saying we would see each other later. So dad, of course, caught him right before he was coming to the window. Mom was banging on my door, and Dad called the cops and said that he was sneaking in my window, but we were in love.

He and his family went back to New York at the end of junior year when all that went on. That's when my parents first took me to therapy because they felt something was wrong with me. I think what I did was kind of normal, but they took me to therapy. I'm glad they did though, because it really helped me to start maturing and learning things about myself.

The week before my eighteenth birthday, I had planned to call my high school sweetheart in New York because I still loved him. I called him on my birthday, since there could be no more question of statutory rape. He said he still loved me. That next month, he drove all the way down from New York. He stayed with a friend, and we decided we wanted to get married. We married on December 9, just a couple months later.

It was a disaster. He was immature and smoked a lot of

weed. I was working and he would go to work sometimes. Other times he would say he was at work, but I'd come home from my job and find him there with a friend, smoking. He wasn't my type at all. He was kind of rude and arrogant, so I left him several times and went back to my parents. My dad would come, pack up my stuff, and we would go.

We got divorced, but he would come begging, saying he would change, and he'd cry and say he loved me so much, so we married again.

The reason we did this is because I couldn't shack up. My dad wouldn't support me or help me keep going to college if I lived with a man out of wedlock, so I had to marry him. So I was married again, and then in my immaturity I decided it'd be better if I got pregnant and had a baby. That would really mature us and bring us together! So, I got pregnant, but nothing changed and we divorced a second time while I was pregnant.

He wasn't there when Sierra was born. Then after she was born, when she was eight months old, **we married again**!

Yes, I married the same immature, arrogant, mean guy three times! But this time I only stayed with him a month. Sierra was eight months old, and I married him again because he said he had changed and was going to be mature. When I saw that first month that he had not changed at all, I left, got more therapy, and never looked back.

He did go on to marry another woman and they ended up spending I think about thirteen years together and have four more children. He never was a part of Sierra's life growing up.

There are three things I want to say about this. First, while my dad was a good dad, both of my parents were hypocritical and unreasonable about purity. For one thing, they had sex before marriage. I know this is why they were so strict, but still, the idea that I could have been capable of doing what they were not capable of is nonsense. By that point, my mother had already proven herself to be below standard when it came to sexual morals. The idea that it would be better to be married to my ex simply because we couldn't control ourselves is fundamentally flawed. Though the *Bible* teaches this *on some level,* the context for a betrothed Israelite is very different for an American teenager who is dating somebody. It was a mistake on my father's part to make me marry the very same man whom he had called the police on. That kind of controlling parenting can only ever lead to rebellion.

The second thing is that I wanted to really express the level of brokenness in my life at that point. I wanted you to see it because I have overcome it with God's help and therapy.

That brings up the third point. The bright spot in those times was that I began a life of seeking self-knowledge in therapy. I'll write more on this in later chapters, but it was a good thing.

No matter where you are, there is hope for healing and maturing. I hope if nothing else, you get that from my story.

Chapter 5

Mothering (Everyone)

"Experience is a hard teacher because she gives the test first, the lesson afterwards." -Vernon Sanders Law

IF YOU DON'T COUNT THAT I had to mother my mother and father when I was a teenager, I consider myself to have become a mom when I was eighteen years old. My mom's baby brother struggled with drug addiction and he had a son with a woman with the same challenge who he met in rehab. In spring of 1990, I was there when their child was born.

I have always loved children and started babysitting when I was eleven years old, so when my uncle and his wife struggled, I took the baby in and raised him off and on from the time he was two months old. His mother would go off on binges, and I'd help my uncle. Besides my parents, this was the first deep love I had for another being. He was like my own child.

My uncle had been an addict for most of his life from the time he was around thirteen years old. When my little cousin's mom was clean, he'd live with her, but as soon as she fell off the wagon, he'd be back with me. Sadly, his father died when he was five from a double hernia operation.

He was a constant in my life, and when he needed help, I helped him. When he fell behind in school, I tutored him. When he needed braces, I got them for him. He grew up and went into the military, and when he got out, he came back "home" to live with us. He moved out after a while, but then came back off and on whenever he needed support. He worked for us for a while in our family business.

I also had my own daughter during that time. I married the first time at eighteen, and a little over a year later was pregnant with my daughter, Sierra. At age twenty, on New Year's Day (interestingly, she shares a birthday with my father, who was the Baby New Year of 1951), I became a new mother.

After a horrific natural delivery, I swore I'd never go through that again! Sadly, I was already divorced by the time my daughter was born. My marriage had been hard already, and pregnancy didn't help. After that, Sierra and I lived with my parents again.

Sierra came out of the womb with a tough, type A personality. Now at thirty, she's still that way. She cried a lot and was colicky, so those early days were hard. I was also going to school at the same time to get my nursing degree. During that time, I met the wonderful man who has been my husband now *for* nearly thirty years. Two years later, I got pregnant again, and this time had a C-section, having made a vow never to go through what I did the first time. Tristan, my son, was born with a mild, reserved personality, taking after my sweet husband, though now that he's older, I can see a lot more of myself in him.

With my little cousin in and out of our home through those years, I had three children to raise, and it seemed like a lot. I was never able to take birth control, because it really messed up my moods and hormones, so Joe had a vasectomy when Tristan was a month old. We both thought we were done having kids.

Six years later, I started to find myself wanting another child. The mother in me missed having babies and toddlers around. By then our income was a little more stable, so Joe agreed we could adopt a child. After looking into it, we decided to adopt from China.

Though we were more stable, we did not have the kind of funds needed to adopt from overseas, but I truly believed adoption was something God was calling us to do. First, I had a strange situation where I continually ran into the same woman in a nearby town who had adopted a beautiful Asian girl. At the same time, the Christian artist Steven Curtis Chapman promoted adoption at every one of his concerts.

Then, my best friend's sister got a job as a nanny for a couple. As she described the beautiful little girl she watched, I realized it was the same family who had adopted their daughter from Asia somewhere. I ran into her again at the Social Security office, then again at the grocery store. I had never seen the woman in my life, and then suddenly I was seeing and hearing of her all the time. It felt like a God thing and that he was confirming what was in my heart.

Within six weeks of looking into the process, things came together. I said, "Okay God, we don't have the money to do this, but I'm just going to step out and do it."

My husband and I were both believers by this time, and we had taken risks prior to that in business, so why not take a risk on this? So, we went for it. We scraped up the money for the initial application through an adoption agency called Great Wall of China. As happens every time we step out in faith, money just started showing up. We got a weird and unexpected refund in the mail from a house we had sold. Then it was a refund on some insurance premium we had overpaid. It amounted to $4,000 and blew our minds.

We were then able to send our dossier to China, and everything happened in record time. If you've ever known anyone who has tried international adoption, you know this borders on miraculous. We went there immediately and got matched quickly after we had been told to expect a long wait. We got a photo of our precious Mia and we accepted, flying to China a couple of weeks later when she was ten months old. She was our little princess. Then we had Sierra, thirteen, Tristan, eight, and baby Mia.

I thought for sure we were done having kids and that it was time to focus on building our business, but then at forty years old, I heard God tell me to have another child. At this point, there are two things you ought to know about me. Number one, I have always wanted a big family. I'm sure you gathered that by now. Number two may be less obvious. I can tend to run off without God and seek to accomplish things with my own strength. I have abilities and a bias for making things happen. I'm a natural networker and a go-getter. In business, I can head up huge events and connect people with one another, and I have a reputation in these networks as the go-to person for pretty much anything. You need your dog groomed? I know a guy. An architect, a painter, a doctor, a therapist? Whatever, I know everybody. I know if they are good. I know if they are not. But this is often my downfall, and sometimes I can get ahead of God, rushing forward without quite checking with him about his plan. I struggle with patience, and I've had to learn the hard way again and again that if I would simply slow down and do it God's way by waiting for him, things would go infinitely smoother.

Adoption Nightmare

This next adoption when I was forty-one was no different. I had connections—I knew a woman. I checked into fostering and stateside adoptions, and I practically forced my husband to go with me to an attorney who advertised that he would save babies from prison. Their mothers were incarcerated and would decide to adopt out their babies to keep them from foster care. That was the route I decided we needed to go. I called my connection and got matched with a mother. A non-refundable $3,000 check was required, and I just paid it to get the process started. Then the mother changed her mind. Our money was gone, and we were back at square one.

That was a wakeup call. At that point I knew I needed to slow down, listen to God, and listen to my husband. I would take time and pray about it. All along, my husband Joe had been wanting us to go through the fostering to adoption route, but I hadn't been willing to entertain the idea until that point, realizing this was God's plan all along. I took a deep breath and attempted to trust God and Joe, even though the fostering route scared me to death. I was afraid of the government, the parents, and the unknown. I had such a hard time with Greg Jr. as his mother came in, out, back in, and back out of his life for years, I didn't want to go through anything like that again. It was scary to me to think about dealing with people and their addictions and issues.

When I finally heard the voice of God, I was lying in a hammock at a health retreat, and I heard him say, "You're going to have more children."

Two months later, we had flown through the foster care class with flying colors. Joe and I are both high achievers, so we approach everything to win, and we did well at the classes. Everything they asked us to do—show up, fill out paperwork, anything—I was the first to do it. I was motivated! And then came the kids.

I was told that one to two newborns a week were born in our county in need of foster care. I thought, "This is going to be great! Easy!"

We quickly had our first newborn and fell in love with him, but after just four months he went back to his family. Shortly after that, I got two newborns at the same time. My husband thought I was crazy. One of them ended up going to an aunt, but the other one I kept. He had part of our family name in his, and I thought, "Wow! This must be God!"

Quickly thereafter, we got a call that a two-year-old needed to stay with us for the weekend until the grandmother could take him on Monday. Well, by Monday, the grandmother remembered she was too old to raise another child (plus, she worked twelve-hour shifts as a nurse), and they said he would stay with us until his mother got herself clean. It turned out that he had been abandoned and malnourished in a house all alone because his mother was in the hospital giving birth to his sister, who was born tiny, sickly, and addicted to drugs. They had to have the poor thing on a morphine drip for several months to get her off the drugs.

My heart had been broken a month earlier when the first baby went back to his family, and they moved to another county. It's hard to describe how sad and low I was then. I felt like I'd been stabbed a hundred times in the stomach with a knife. I could barely take all of this pain and depravity.

I worried myself sick about the baby and how he was doing, but there was one bright spot. It meant I had room for two more children, so when the little baby sister could leave the hospital, we got her, too. I loved those babies so much, but what a heartbreaking situation. The visitations were terrible; waiting two hours for their parents to maybe not show up, or maybe show up high and strung out, passing their drug tests with a bag of urine inside their body cavity. The mother told me this once, arrogantly, and then of course denied it. This went on for over a year.

The state was going to allow all the kids to go back to their families, even though we knew they were still abusing drugs and lying about it. We were not going to stand by and allow that injustice and the state's incredible negligence and stupidity to ruin the lives of these kids. Our state gives monthly stipends for each child every month that you foster, plus free healthcare while they're growing up and even college tuition. But we gave that up and decided to go to court to fight DCFS for our kids. We hired a private investigator to catch the parents using drugs, and $47,000 later, we won our case and officially became the parents of "the Littles," J, A, and N. I was forty-two years old with two one-year-olds, a three-year-old, and "the Bigs," Mia and Tristan (Sierra was grown). Wow! I never thought I'd end up with that many children! But I was very happy, in my element, and living my best life.

Mothering is just what I do; it's who I am. I, of course, mother my children, but I mother my parents, my friends, or even a stranger I'm meeting for the first time. If someone seems to need nurturing, every part of me just shows up. If a problem needs to be solved that will make someone's life better, I'm all in!

I'm a Turkey!

I heard the other day about the mothering instinct in turkeys and how their instincts can get triggered. They said that mother turkeys will attack a skunk that comes anywhere near their babies. They bring out their claws and beaks, and they become vicious, absolutely aiming to kill that perceived predator. A group of researchers got a fake skunk and pulled it with a string up to the turkey and her chicks. She went ballistic and tried to kill the stuffed animal.

That makes sense, doesn't it? That's what we mothers do. We protect our young, but what happened next was truly astonishing. The researchers took the very same stuffed skunk and inserted in it a device that made a chirping sound like a baby turkey. This time the researchers dragged the skunk toward the mom and chicks, but with that chirping sound coming out of it.

Guess what happened? The turkey gathered the little fake skunk under her wing *with her babies!* The chirping sound triggered an instinct that caused the turkey to lose her mind! Don't tell the skunks they can trick the turkeys so easily. It'll be open season on baby turkey chicks!

Interestingly, just as soon as they removed the chirping device from the fake skunk, the mother turkey went back to trying to kill it!

I am just like that momma turkey. What triggers me? Anyone, and I mean anyone, who needs help or nurturing. Let me see you hurting, hungry, in some kind of need, and I'm your momma! Can you relate?

This nurturing instinct is all well and good, if and only if you realize it and develop some wisdom about it. You don't want to be that turkey inviting skunks under your wing to destroy your household. You must have discernment.

Parenting my Parents

For me, the real challenge is to not parent my parents. Look, there comes a time in every life when children have to begin to take care of their elderly parents. It's part of the reason to have kids in the first place—so there will be someone there when you get old. First, you have to work some things out, or you will take this responsibility in a sinful way. I have seen many people, when their parents get old and helpless, start to be borderline abusive to them. Why does this happen? I think it is because there are a whole bunch of unresolved resentments. People don't say what needs to be said when they need to say it, so they retaliate by mistreating their moms and dads.

Think of it as a generational cycle. Many of our mothers found themselves resenting us as kids. My mom grew up in the generation of women's lib. She got pregnant and married very young. She did love me, but she always wanted something more than what she got. The way she treated me was a result of that, especially after the first time she left and came back.

By the time I grew up, I had built up considerable resentment towards her in return. Also, there is this spiritual phenomenon when it comes to parents passing on their sins to their children. The Bible is clear on the issue. It is so important to deal with our junk so we don't pass it on to our kids. Let's just say my mother passed on some spiritual baggage, and I tend to take it out on her. The only way for me to forgive her and not be harsh with my words to her is to know that I have been direct and said what needs to be said. I have to set boundaries and not permit my mother (or my father) to take advantage of me, I will discuss this further in Chapter 8.

Most people are not direct. They are afraid to be direct, to say "no," to set boundaries. Instead, they harbor resentment and retaliate when their parents get too old and feeble to fight back.

Mothering My Dad

I want now to take a brief moment to bring up my dad in the context of people in my life who I find myself mothering. While this is a book about my mother, I don't want to make it seem like there are no issues with my dad. First, the good.

Some of it I have mentioned already. My dad was wonderful to me as a little girl. I was definitely a daddy's girl. At the same time, he worked a lot and wasn't around much. My dad modeled hard work, but he also spent a lot of money, leaving us struggling financially much of the time.

He was also the strict one. I don't waver very much from how my dad raised me. As a little girl, I liked that he was stricter than my mom. It felt safe that he didn't let me run around and he gave me values. When it came to sleeping around, I was never that kind of girl. When it came to respect for authority, I was raised old school. "Yes ma'am," and "No ma'am." Elbows off the table, chew with your mouth closed. When you play with your toys, put them away. When you wake up, make your bed. Especially when I saw my mom going down a bad path, I wanted to be more like my dad.

However, today, I am more of a mother to my dad at times, and it can be hard. My parents finally quit getting back together and my dad got remarried to—are you ready for this? He married my husband's mother! My dad and my husband's mom are married. This has been a source of tension at times, but over the years it has become a more normal feeling.

Beyond that, our constant argument concerns his health. He tells me he can't do anything, but then tells the doctors and nurses that he's doing fine. They tell him he needs to lose weight, and he promises he will. Unfortunately, he still eats terribly and doesn't get up from the couch very often.

That's all well and good until I try to take responsibility for it; until I try to be his mother. This is where my mothering instinct gets the best of me. When I see someone, really *anyone*, in some kind of need, every part of me perks up, *especially* if I think I have the solution. Oh, if they would only listen to me! You cannot take responsibility for someone else's choices. I mean, I'm still trying to take control of my own choices on a daily basis. I need to learn that today, even as I write this.

On the one hand, I have great resources and wisdom. I'm smiling because I sound like I'm bragging, but I'm just saying that I have fought long and hard to know what I know and to have what I have. You know the old *Spider-Man* quote from Uncle Ben? "With great power comes great responsibility."

That is true. It is also biblical.

This responsibility emerges from the fact that we are put here by God to accomplish his purposes for us. We're told the incredible news that we are created in his image. Imagine you had a lot you wanted to get done. Imagine you had the ability to multiply yourself and deploy all the copies of yourself to be productive. This is exactly what God has done. He made us with the capacity and drive to work. He gave us gifts and talents and skills, and he said to use these to have dominion over the Earth and all that is in it. God said to *produce*. He said to *multiply*. This means to reproduce, but it also means to make things grow. Make crops grow. Make businesses grow.

Make nations grow. God put us here to grow. It is thrilling to think about the massive potential in each and every one of us!

Of course, he has given all the image-bearers free will, so this is where it gets tricky. Jesus shows the difference between the three servants; the three image-bearers of the master left behind to do his work. They didn't all rise to the challenge, which is a tragedy. The one with the greatest ability took what he had been given and made the most he could of it. That was the servant with five talents. The next had less ability to start with, but he took what he had and made the very most of it. People love to wallow in victimhood by comparing themselves with others who are "better" than them at something, but this man didn't.

This victim attitude can create a vicious and crippling sense of entitlement that causes people to be like the third steward in the story who was given something to work with but did *nothing* with it.

Now, if I, Mamma Sabrina, was the five-talent servant, and I saw the one-talent servant, I'd want to waste a bunch of time and emotional energy trying to shore him up. I'd say, "I feel sorry for you. Here, have some of my talents."

Then I'd be heartbroken when he'd inevitably squander that too, along with his original bag with one talent. Wait a minute, aren't we supposed to be faithful with what we've been given? Is it not faithful to enable the one-talent guy? Shouldn't I just take care of him since God has given me the talent to do so?

No!

How can we balance all of this? The fact is, it's wonderful to help people, but enabling them by mothering does not give them the leg up they need to go and produce. That's not how it works, because that is not how God created his people to work. There is only a very tiny minority of humanity that must be cared for by someone else. The very ill, the completely and utterly handicapped, and babies. Anyone who can stand all day long on the street corner looking sad (and usually overly fed) with a cardboard sign can also go and work. Some people even get paid to hold those signs!

My greatest temptation is to feel guilty for what God has given me. It is right to see everything you have as a gift, but you also have everything by cause and effect. Even when Jesus promises that God will give you everything, the promise comes with an "if/then" statement.

Steep your life in God-reality, God-initiative, God-provisions. Don't worry about missing out. You'll find all your everyday human concerns will be met.

> "Give your entire attention to what God is doing right
> now, and don't get worked up about what may
> or may not happen tomorrow."
> —Matthew 6:33-34a

God has a kingdom. You are created as an image-bearing steward of that kingdom and put into the midst of that kingdom to do your part. What is your part? Stewarding what God has given you. You say he hasn't given you anything? Wrong!

First of all, you are reading this. That means he has given you a mind that is capable of doing amazingly complex things like reading. No other living thing can read because the abstraction required is only possible for us image-bearers.

Second, you have a body to steward. How is that going? Whatever health level you are at can almost always be improved. Stewardship of the body requires you to be attentive to the priceless resource that is your body. Get enough sleep, eat healthy food, and exercise.

Third, you have financial resources. "Nuh-uh," you say, "I'm poor."

You are not destitute. Start living beneath your means. Get to work. Start paying down debt. You can do it. Learn skills that add value to other people so you can get paid. Create more than you consume.

You have relationships to steward. You have experiences to steward. You have wisdom. You may not be considered wise because maybe you have not lived according to the wisdom you have. *But the minute you start living wisely, you are wise.*

You have free will. You have the invitation to abide in Christ. You have so much. You have everything. You have reconciliation with God. You have peace through Jesus. You have forgiveness. You have heaven in your future. You have the potential for an incredible life if you will only understand these foundational truths.

Now...

What must you not do? You must not enable others. You can certainly tell them the truth. You can encourage them with the Word. You can call them out for failing to live up to the great potential God has given them, but you cannot do it for them.

You can lead a horse to water, but you cannot make them drink, and trying to make them drink will come to no end of frustration.

This is what I need to work on. Yes, with great power comes great responsibility, but that *does not mean taking responsibility for someone else.* My friend Jeff says it means being responsible *to* them, not *for* them. How can you do this?

Set an example. Live your wise life before them and don't let them say you were blessed with some opportunity that they weren't. Friends and family say to me, "I'm not like you. You're lucky to be the way you are."

Only be willing to help anyone who is willing to do their part. This is not cruel. It is cruel not to require them to do their part. They are not functioning as image-bearers if they are not doing their part. This will lead them to misery, and it will be partly your fault for enabling them.

Do not, do not, do not reward someone for hurting you. Do not allow someone to treat you any other way than lovingly and fairly. What did Jesus say the master said to the wicked and lazy servant? Get to the outer darkness! He told his disciples to brush the dust off and leave the town that did not want to accept responsibility for the truth.

You may feel guilty, especially if you have people in your life you've allowed to use guilt-tripping on you. If you were raised on guilt, this could take some work. Unearned guilt is a big problem for most people. Guilt is fine if you've done something wrong. Repent, and turn back to Jesus. If you still feel guilt after doing that, then tell Satan to shut up and go away.

My mothering instinct was put to good use when it caused me to have and adopt children. It's helping me to raise them and raise them right. However, it is not helpful when it comes to those God has not called me to mother.

One other thing, if you happen to be a man reading this, and you find yourself guilty of these things, don't make the mistake of thinking you aren't mothering too. Don't mistake what you're doing as fathering. We'll save the word "fathering" for what God does with us. I know that it is stereotypical, but traditionally, a father will give a bit of tougher love. A father will train up a child, but then give them their independence and enough rope to let them fail. They will come alongside and encourage, but not take over the will of the child. That's a perfect father, and of course, none of us had one of those. Even my dad, as flawed as he may be, reflected the heavenly Father well in this way. So men, don't you be mothering everyone either.

Let me help you, as I still remind myself of these things all the time. Receive these words: *Go free, in Jesus' name, of mothering, of taking responsibility for others. Hold even your own kids with open hands to the Lord.*

Chapter 6

Serenity Prayer—What Can You Change and What Must You Accept?

God grant me the serenity to accept
The things I cannot change..
The courage to change the things I can..
And the wisdom to know the difference.

THERE ARE VERY FEW STATEMENTS that are more powerful and truthful than the Serenity Prayer. I've prayed these words a thousand times when it comes to my mother. Ever since I was a young wife, I've hung that prayer up in my house where I could see it every day and let the words shape me. I wanted to use this chapter to think about this a little deeper.

O God…

I've already made it plain that God is the source of all good in my life. He is the healer, the truth bearer, the creator of all things good. He is my perfect parent who loves me, who keeps his promises, and who never fails me.

Grant to me…

Every desirable and beneficial gift comes out of heaven. (James 1:17). Even when we work for the things we have, it is right and good to thank God for providing for us, because our hard work doesn't have to pay off. Our investments, wise as we think we are, don't have to profit us. Our health can fail, bank accounts can run dry, our efforts could be futile. We live in a fallen world where God promised Adam that his work would be hard because of the fall. Many people work hard in vain, so when our effort pays off, we thank God. Are you a hard worker?

The serenity of mind…

Serenity of mind comes from God and it is real. A friend of mine had come from a spiritually abusive church network that could easily be defined more as a cult than a church. He had been dominated and abused for fifteen years until he stood up to the leaders and spoke out against their abusive practices. They were the kind of leaders who not only led a horse to water, but also forced him to drink.

By God's grace, my friend was healed of the effects of those wounds, but when he applied for another ministry position, the interviewers were unable to believe that he could be emotionally and spiritually healthy after what he'd been through. He explained over and over how Jesus had first given him the understanding that the way he was being led was wrong, then he'd given him the strength to leave, and then forgive his abusers. After that, Jesus healed the wounds so that he could once again fellowship with church networks and congregations without being triggered, and finally Jesus had restored in him the joy of the Lord. These interviewers had one question. "Have you been to therapy?"

Now, I think that everyone can benefit from the self-discovery that results from time with a good therapist. But would I say that Jesus is lying when the *Bible* says that God can grant us peace supernaturally? Of course not! Serenity of mind comes from the Lord. Even if you find peace partially by doing therapeutic work, it still comes from the Lord, and we should pray for this gift even as we seek it.

To accept that which cannot be changed…

What can't be changed about your life? It's not always an easy question to answer, is it? But sometimes it is. You cannot make yourself taller. You can make yourself *appear* taller with platform shoes, until you turn an ankle. You cannot change your past. You can't make things un-happen. You can change your attitude about them, but we'll talk about that in a few moments.

You can't change who your family is. You can't change (very easily) what the government is doing. You can't change the global economy. You can't change your race, and I'm sorry to tell some people, but you can't change your sex. There are all kinds of things you cannot change. For our purposes, I'd love to help you get it through your head that you cannot change other people! I can't even change you with this book!

In my own life, tempted to mother everyone, I'm often under the illusion that I can change someone. To be sure, you can help people. You can show them a better way, but they are the ones who have to do all the changing. Even if you think you are the one changing someone, you probably are not changing them at all. At best, you are getting them to pretend to change in order to make you happy. If anyone is going to truly change, they have to be the ones to do it.

File this concept in the category of things you cannot change and must accept. You must accept that people are how they are. My mother is not going to change. She isn't. She isn't! (Oh sorry, you caught me yelling at myself). I cannot change my mom or dad no matter how hard I try or how bad I want to. At very best, I can manage how they treat me by setting good boundaries (more on this later). I must accept that they are how they are.

There is a difference between accepting that someone is the way they are and accepting them *as* they are. You have to accept that they are the way they are. You don't have to accept them at all. You can accept that someone is awful to you, that you can't change that fact, and then lovingly put them out of your life. Even if it is your mother.

It's hard, though. How do you know when that is the right option? I said before that you can change how they treat you by setting good boundaries.

My friend Jeff's mother is narcissistic and, bless her heart, makes everything about her. She's insecure and spends all her time gossiping to one sibling about another and laying guilt trips and shame to get her four kids to do what she wants them to do.

One day, Jeff came to the conclusion that he would have a good relationship with his mother or no relationship at all. He had to accept that he could not change her fundamentally, but maybe he could get her to keep his rules around him and his family.

One day they were talking on the phone, and his mother started to gossip about a sibling. Jeff questioned, "Mom, does (sibling) know you are telling me that?"

She paused, then said, "Well, no."

Jeff exclaimed, "Would you want them to know you told me?"

"Well, no."

"Then don't tell me and actually, I don't want you to share confidential information with me about anyone else."

Jeff's mother was triangulating that way all the time. Jeff knew that as soon as they got off the phone that she would likely be calling his siblings to talk about him. He didn't actually care about that. He knew who he was, and they could talk if they wanted, but he didn't feel right about playing along anymore.

His mother was furious. First, she got quiet and said she had to go. Jeff didn't protest. He knew she would be waiting for him to call her back and apologize. He didn't. Two days went by, and she called crying and saying how bad he'd hurt her, and that she had to talk to him about that stuff because he was so wise and she had to talk to *someone* about it.

He responded that it was gossip, sinful, and a cheap way to build connection between people, also a cheap way to build herself up. She never understood his argument. She never changed her opinion about it, even though she admitted she wouldn't want anyone talking about her in that way. She did, however, promise not to gossip to him anymore.

Jeff and his mother had a similar interaction over the guilt she placed on him as a method to get him to do what she wanted. He told her she had guilted him into action all his life, and he would no longer put up with it. He also told her how he felt screwed up by her, and that if she wanted a relationship with him and his family, she would follow the rules. Not only would he ignore her guilt trips, but he would also pull away if she tried that tactic in the future. This conversation worked because in the end, she believed him. He knows she hasn't changed her interactions with everyone else, but she behaves almost perfectly around him.

When you can't change someone (which is never ever), you have to accept that they are the way they are and decide what you will do. First, try to set boundaries, and if that doesn't work then just walk away.

This example with Jeff's mom is a big one, but often it's the little ones that ruin people's day. Think of the many stupid little things that happen to upset you during the day. Someone is driving crazy in traffic. It's not personal, but you take it that way and get road rage over something you can't change. Why? Instead, accept it as part of driving. One of two things is going on with that driver. One, they are in a dire situation and have to get somewhere fast, or more likely, they are an irresponsible person. If that is true, they are probably reaping all sorts of consequences in their life. You don't have to worry that they are getting away with anything. Nobody gets away with anything in this world of cause and effect. Eventually, they will get pulled over. If they are irresponsible on the road, they are irresponsible in other places too. Let God worry about that.

As for you, embrace the freedom of accepting what can't be changed. Believe that God is on his throne and completely aware. Believe that the Bible is true when it says, "He knows us far better than we know ourselves, knows our pregnant condition, and keeps us present before God. That's why we can be so sure that every detail in our lives of love for God is worked into something good" (Romans 8:28).

What if we saw all the things that happen which are out of our control as a way for God to take something bad and turn it into a way for us to grow?

Life is all about the next challenge. You can't prevent some things from happening, but you can decide how you are going to respond. Will you accept the trial and use it, or will you be set back by it, playing the victim and giving up? God will grant you the serenity to accept what can't be changed, but even better, he can help you to benefit from it.

Courage to change that which can be changed...

To get the most mileage out of our example above, consider Jeff's situation with his mother. You might be thinking, "That dude is stone cold."

Nope, he was terrified. His mother could not be changed, but one of two things could be changed: either he could change the way she behaved toward him, or he could change the fact that she was in his life at all. But this required him to defy every nerve in his body. He'd been carefully trained by his mom to fear her reactions. To his nervous system, upsetting his mom would mean his death. It sounds silly, but you learn those kinds of things when you are less than two years old when your sense of self is formed.

When Jeff was just realizing that he was an autonomous person, there was this important woman with a storm of emotions. When you're two, you think you are the center of the universe, so if your mother or father is emotional, especially if they seem to be upset with you, you naturally think it must be your fault. You learn that you have to make this person happy all the time. Your life and identity depend on it!

What a way to mess up a kid. Jeff reversed this deep-seated feeling finally at the age of forty-four, when he became a different person by choosing another way. Making that choice, having the *courage* to make that choice, actually changed him. It was brutal, but following through on it actually changed him by changing his nervous system. He is now a different type of person. For Jeff, this was a God thing. Action is one of those things that makes a difference, because God created us to change by first acting in the new way, then becoming the kind of person who acts that way.

Why are we afraid to change? We're afraid because our body tells us a lie about what will happen if we do the right but scary thing. It feels like we will die. **But we will not die. We will adapt.** Taking a tough stand is hard and requires courage, because we have to have faith that *after* the deed is done, we will reap the benefit of becoming different.

"Death" is not a bad way to look at it; however, maybe I should not say "we will not die," because a part of us will die. But it will be the part or parts that need to die. What is reborn then is a *version of us* that is more authentically who God created and is creating. Christians believe that we are being transformed from the moment we give our lives to Christ. We believe God sees what our potential is, what we are going to become when Jesus returns, what we will look like at the sound of the last trumpet when we are changed in the blink of an eye. Death of the old self is really the right way to think of it.

The serenity prayer is used in Alcoholics Anonymous for a reason. It takes courage to change a life of alcoholism. It takes courage to wake up every day and say no to the escape of substance abuse. If we are not escaping, then we are facing every minute of the reality of our lives.

"That which can be changed" is anything related to our own behavior. Overly clever social scientists like to yap about determinism and say that people are raised a certain way, with a certain temperament and they really shouldn't have to face the consequences of their actions, because they can't help it. But if that is true, we are in grave danger.

It's not true, however. You must fight to believe that you can change. If you have courage, you will become a different person—a better, more honest, more courageous, healthier version of yourself. Let me make you a promise:

If you will ask God for the necessary courage to change, he will give it to you.

What needs to change? Who do you need to stand up to? Who do you need to say "no" to and stop enabling? Who do you need to forgive or seek forgiveness from? What toxic behaviors do you need to lay at the feet of Jesus? Where do you need to change? Don't worry if you aren't sure. Ask God and start with what you know. He'll give you what you need, and afterward, you will truly be a different version of yourself.

And the wisdom to know the one from the other...

This was sort of implied in the above paragraphs, but it requires a little bit of fleshing out. How do you know what you can and cannot change? I submit to you that you do know. The knowledge is deep down, but it's there. When you slow down and talk with Jesus, you are in a place to start looking deep for his peace. Ask yourself questions. Rather than anxiety, even the hard truth produces peace if you are ready to accept it.

Running from the truth creates fear, anxiousness, and inner conflict. Sadly, many people avoid knowing the truth because they think dealing with it will be hard. It will be hard, but only for a short time, then an unbelievable sense of peace will descend. That "wisdom to know" the difference between what you should change and what you should accept is found where peace lies.

I find myself at fifty years old and ready to commit to writing this book that has been on my heart for over ten years now. It's amazing how faithfully God surprises me when I get calm, quiet down, and stop participating in the busyness and chaos. That's when I can hear and feel the wonderful things that he has for my life. I have tended to stay so busy and so caught up in the tasks and things that need to get done that I forget to pause and enjoy the goodness around me. That state of living is when I miss what has been the true calling on my life.

Do you know what needs to change? Do you know what needs to be accepted? I believe you already know but ask God anyway so he can draw it from within you. Say this prayer: "Lord, show me the difference. Let me experience peace as I approach the truth of a situation. Give me everything I need to be able to accept what I can't change but change what I can. In Jesus' name, Amen."

Chapter 7

Mothering Yourself—Why Exhaustion and Self-Loathing Isn't The Solution to Being a Good Mom

"A Woman's Work is Never Done"

I GET OVERWHELMED and exhausted sometimes. There are so many feelings, emotions, dreams, and failures wrapped up in the role of being a mother and figuring out how to navigate through life. It's a challenge to find happiness and health and become your own true individual self when you're trying to be something that doesn't always come naturally, which is the perfect mom. Who wants to be a bad mom or a mom that barely makes it through the day? We all want to do the best that we can, but to have another's life in our hands is a lot of pressure, so we push and push ourselves.

Add to our internal pressure the nasty business of comparison with other moms. Not only do we compare with the moms we know, but we also compare ourselves to the highly curated versions of these moms on social media and blogs, where people only put the enviable things in their lives for the world to see, and half of the time they are faking it.

I know there are men out there that feel that same pressure, and they do great with their children. But there is such a hard and high expectation for a mother's role in a child's life. I was raised old school. The husbands went out and worked a lot, and they were to be respected. The women raised the children. They cooked and cleaned and bathed them. They took them to dentist appointments and the orthodontist and to get their shots before school. These mothers sat down and ordered new backpacks, shopped for school supplies and clothing, and tried on all the shoes to find the right pair to start school. They purchased all the Christmas presents. A lot fell on the mom's shoulders. Let's face it, we are Santa Claus, the Easter Bunny, the Tooth Fairy, supermom, cheerleaders, and math tutors. I mean, where does it end? Aside from all of these roles, who is mom? I can tell you one thing, she is exhausted.

Do We Have to Be Exhausted?

The question remains: Is exhaustion something to accept or change? Well, it's all relative and has a lot to do with the stage of life you're in. If you have babies and they don't sleep through the night yet, well, hang on, you can handle anything for a little while. Just don't make it worse than it has to be. Take care of yourself the best you can. It'll get better. Be smart about what you do when the baby is napping. Don't just start cleaning the house every time they nap. Know when you need to nap, too.

Do you take time to sit down and read a book or take a cat nap? Or are you spending every second doing the laundry, wiping the counters again, dusting the furniture, sweeping off the porch—just constantly working? That was one of the biggest mistakes that I made. I was constantly working. Every time I could have gotten a break, I did not take it. All the family gatherings were at our house because our house was the hub. I just worked and worked and worked—for every cookout, every holiday. I worked for days before, preparing for cooking. Then the day of the gathering, most of the time, I spent it in the kitchen cooking, helping pack the food up, and cleaning up the mess, and *then* I'd sit down. The event was over thirty minutes after I finished all of that work, and everybody would go home. I missed out on the time I could have spent with my guests and felt exhausted. I worked to make it so nice for everybody else, but I didn't really spend much time with my family. They all got together and talked to each other while I slaved away.

Through the years, I ended up resenting having those gatherings, and now I don't even want to have gatherings as often because I don't want to put that pressure on myself. I'll have pressure to perform, and I don't have any way around that. I still struggle to find that balance. As I write this, my birthday is this coming Sunday, and I woke up to a text this morning from my daughter saying, "We didn't know if you were going to be in town, but since you're in town, do you want us all to get together at your house?"

My initial instinct was, "I don't think so."

I don't think that I want to do that because I'm worn out, and I don't want to be even more exhausted after I somehow have to throw a party for myself.

It's hard to balance that out as a woman and a mom. I'm not completely sure how it is for a man. I've been told that men are more prone to see their "work" as something they do somewhere else, or during "work hours." They don't feel the same kind of pressure, but if you are a wife and mom, especially if you are a stay-at-home mom, there is no separation between home and work, and it is very difficult to stop.

For me, the only time I ever felt it was okay to stop was bedtime. That was the reward. I always loved when I would tuck the babies in. I'd get myself ready for bed. I'd have candles (I don't do candles anymore since I've discovered they suck oxygen out of the room), and everything would be spotless. Music would be playing low. I'd love to go to sleep at night because I'd earned my rest. Maybe I'd hear the dryer going because I was finishing laundry, and everything was clean. That was such a rewarding feeling. I loved it. I felt a satisfying sense of accomplishment having gotten everything done. The next day I'd start over again, but I regret that back then I didn't insert more routines to pause like that during the day; more reasons to stop and rest.

Now, I approach it differently. If you're still in that stage, I hope I can convince you that it is not only okay to add some moments of rest in your daily routines. It is actually crucial for your own wellbeing. We're built to run on cycles. Have you noticed that during some times of the day you are charged up, sharp (assuming your babies are letting you sleep at night), and you can be productive? Yet at other times, have you noticed how you can't finish a sentence because you forget what you were talking about? You try to read something, and you blank out six times in one paragraph? Figure out what your most productive time of day is and then use it to make the most progress. Find your least motivational time and plan to use that as your rest and recovery time. Using your strengths and weaknesses to your advantage works out best for all in the long run.

Think of how God created the body to need sleep every night. Even your sleep comes in cycles. He created seasons so that vegetation even takes a break. If instead of fighting this reality you yield to it, you will find yourself happier and more productive. Exhaustion will not make you a better mom. I promise.

More on Self-Care

While we're at it, let's talk a little more about this concept of self-care. It has become cliche to bring up the example of oxygen masks on airplanes. You have probably heard the instructions and had the same thought I did. The flight attendant tells us that masks will fall from the ceiling when there is an "unexpected drop in cabin pressure." Now say it with me, "If you are traveling with a small child, *put on your own mask first, then help the child with theirs.*"

Why do they say this? Because they know your instinct will be to first help the child.

Why is that not the best way? I know this is obvious, but let's finish the exercise. Imagine you are trying to put the child's mask on, but you pass out first from the effort. The child didn't quite get theirs on either, so you're both down and out.

This really is a perfect metaphor for the way most moms work and think. Don't feel guilty. It's because you care. It's because you are a great mom. But now, listen when I tell you that always looking out for others without taking care of yourself doesn't work.

Think of it logically. What if when you were nursing you never ate because that would feel selfish? You let your babies feed on you, but eventually you would stop producing milk. This is bad for you *and* them, and it applies across many areas, not just breastfeeding.

You are a person with needs. You have a responsibility to God to steward your own life. No one else has this responsibility. He has not charged anyone else with making sure you sustain your life. Your husband may care a lot about you, but the ultimate responsibility for your life is you and God.

In an earlier chapter, we looked at the parable of the talents. Do you know what the one talent is? It is your life. If God gave you nothing else, he gave you your life. If you woke up tomorrow morning in the wilderness, what would be your one job? Staying alive. Consider yourself in the wilderness of motherhood and keeping a home! Staying alive and healthy is not your one job, *but it is your first job!*

You are right that many people rely on you. If you continue in faithful stewardship, you'll probably find that list of dependent people growing. That's how it works. But if people are relying on you, they need you at the top of your game; your pinnacle! Eat, exercise, and do your devotions so you can offer your very best self to your loved ones.

Why aren't you doing this already? Maybe you feel guilty. Were you raised to feel guilty and selfish if you did anything that seemed to benefit you? Maybe your own mom was that way (because, you know, *if it's not one thing it's a mother!*). It is not selfish to take care of yourself. It's *logical*. Who else is going to do it?

A friend of mine was caring for his wife who had thyroid cancer. There is a national conference each year for thyroid cancer and the conference moves around from city to city. One year the conference was taking place not only in their hometown, but it was in a hotel five minutes away from their house. They attended the conference, which was made up of main sessions and optional breakout sessions.

My friend noticed there was a session for the caretakers, so he went to it while his wife went to a different one. My friend genuinely thought the session would be about how to be a better caretaker with tips and skills to learn so he could take better care of his wife.

In reality, the session leader was a therapist who wanted to talk to the caretakers about how to take care of themselves. Having seen that caretakers tend to fall apart eventually because they feel guilty about being healthy and don't think they deserve to care for themselves since, after all, their poor spouses are suffering so much, this therapist saw the need to help the caretakers.

After realizing this, my friend felt panicked, feeling like it was not okay. Eventually, he was convinced that this in fact was a session about how to be a better caretaker. If he was not physically, spiritually, and emotionally healthy, what good would he be to his wife? Hear this story and take it to heart, because the same applies to motherhood.

What are some other reasons you might resist taking time to refresh yourself? Explore these with a counselor or wise older woman. It's important to work this out because being exhausted will not help your kids.

In nursing, I would often see a spouse who was the primary caregiver become the one with failing health. Sometimes it was dementia. They would decline terribly fast. Often they would pass away before the patient did because they would feel they themselves couldn't be laid up in a nursing home or at home with in-home healthcare.

The person that's sick or mentally challenged is getting rest, but the caregiver never is. They often just look worn out, miserable, depressed, and sad—it is all over their faces. They have no quality of life. They feel guilty. Some of them have tons of money. They could have hired somebody to come in to provide some relief, even just for a few hours a day, but they wouldn't, because "what would their kids think?" Realistically, they needed to get out, go to the store, get their nails done, and try to feel human.

You have to deal with the guilt and put it where it belongs.

It is very difficult, but it's okay to say no. Don't just say yes to everything and do everything for everybody. You don't have to be the best neighbor, the best mother, the best daughter, or the best co-worker. You need to be able to be the best YOU, and sometimes that means saying no and putting yourself first.

A Few More Words About Exhaustion

Remember that we are talking about "the courage to change" what can be changed. One of the things that nearly did me in was thinking I had to make sure my kids had every possible opportunity, for fear of them missing out on something. I think a lot of parents make this mistake because they see that other parents are doing it. Thank God I didn't have Facebook when my first daughter was little. That would have done me in. But even then, just knowing that other kids were getting all those opportunities produced anxiety in me, so I'd fill every minute of every day with something.

I had my daughter in dance class, Spanish class, piano lessons, and voice lessons. She was in the children's church on Wednesday nights and of course went to service on Sunday mornings. I had her in pageants; I had her in so many things. Everything that sounded like it would be good or enrich her life or make her amazing, I put her in. I ran myself and her to death between all these different places. That's how we spent our evenings—on the road, some days barely getting back home to do dinner, bath, and homework!

I would not do that now. I do not do that with the kids we still have at home. We pick one thing at a time. They don't have to be in everything.

Steps to Combat Exhaustion

Besides getting out of the parent rat race of participating in every activity, try to set your clock to get up in the morning while it's quiet. One of the biggest breakthroughs for me was when I started waking up before everyone else and taking time to sit down and start my day with meditation. A great place to start is with your favorite devotional book. You can find them everywhere. Then I would pray and receive God's peace at the start of my day. I practiced gratitude and thankfulness simply because I woke up. I thanked God for my life, my home, my husband, and my children. These moments set the pace for the day and started me out right.

Sadly, I went without this for years. I got up right when the alarm went off with all the things I had to do when everybody else was getting up. The kids were getting up, the dog had to go out. Everything was happening at one time. When that pace started my morning, it stayed that way the entire day. I lived in a state of exhaustion and reactivity until I started getting up in the morning when the house was beautiful, quiet, and peaceful. I had time to gather myself through prayer and meditation.

For these times I like guided imagery. If you want a prescription to battle exhaustion, here it is:

Go to bed early.

Set your alarm for an hour, or at least a half hour before anyone else gets up.

When your alarm goes off, remember that you will love this time.

Take some deep breaths, drink some water, and make whatever it is you like to sip on first thing.

Read your devotional for the day and/or a Scripture reading.

Pray. Thank God for the day, for your life, and anything else that comes to mind.

Now, imagine your day and your life the way you want it to go, telling God, "This is my prayer for my day or my life." Imagine how you want to feel, what you want to accomplish, what it will feel like to get it done well. Imagine how you want the rest of the morning to go. How do you want to be? How do you want to love?

Dedicate your day to God and then get on with it.

Committing to this kind of practice changed the whole pace of my day to one that was calmer and more manageable. I would get to work on my tasks but worked more happily with music playing. Nothing was on fire. I guess that's the best way to describe it. I'll admit to you here that one of my friends once said, "Here comes Sabrina. She's always ass on fire!"

It's funny because that's how most of the days went until I got a hold of how to properly start my day. I was just go, go, go, go, go, all day long. Just go! My new morning routine brought calmness where there was none. I still struggle with keeping this in balance. Some days I jump up and rush anyway and find I have an hour to spare before I take the kids to school or head to work. I tend to go towards getting more work done or starting laundry, but I try to take a breath and calm down. I talk to the kids, play music, anything to not feed the racing thoughts of all I need to be doing to be productive. Sometimes NOT being productive is the best medicine for our health.

Budgeting and Focus

My life radically changed when my husband and I learned that we needed to budget our money. Budgeting is knowledge, and knowledge is power. It's awareness. It's having a clue. It's a radical acceptance of reality. I suppose you could make a case for the very rich not needing to budget; but frankly, they need it the most. How many professional athletes make multi-millions of dollars a year only to lose it all in the first year after they are finished playing? Why? Because many of them were raised poor and never developed good spending habits. When they strike it rich, it seems like the money supply is infinite. If their spending stayed the same, it would be like it was infinite, especially if that money was earning interest, but often their spending does not stay the same. It increases to match the paycheck, and then goes beyond it into debt. This is life without awareness. This is life without a budget; without a focus on what is happening.

When you create a budget, the most powerful thing that occurs is that you accept reality. This is something that most people avoid. Many people don't really want to know what is going on. They don't want to know what is happening with their money. If they knew, they might have to put limits on themselves, or accept that they need a better job, or even a second job.

The vast majority of people work hard to keep reality out of focus. They don't want to know. They don't want to know what is going on with their emotions, either. They don't want to deal with whatever makes them anxious or insecure. They don't want to know, so they avoid knowing by medicating or entertaining themselves to death. What I'm saying is worth the price of this book times a million! Get information, peace, and clarity, and see how much better you sleep at night.

Let me make a plug right here for Dave Ramsey's resources, particularly Financial Peace University.[1] Dave's straightforward insights and easy-to-follow baby steps have changed a lot of lives. Any one of his books, if applied, can change your whole financial future.

Do You Feel in Control?

Living on a budget means you operate out of what is true about your financial situation. You will make intelligent decisions and do what you must do to have what you want. Having financial peace is so powerful to me and has a great impact on the way I feel. To be unaware is to be afraid. It can be hard to live a life without fear. If I could do one thing to change your life, it would be to show you how God takes away fear in all its various forms.

I have wasted too much time over the years living in fear. I have spent most of my life fearful about money, or in fear that my parents would pass away, or fearing that something would

---

1   "Financial Peace University," Ramsey Solutions, accessed May 9, 2023, https://www.ramseysolutions.com/ramseyplus/financial-peace?exp=r-plus-49439&gclid=CjwKCAjw3ueiBhBmEiwA4BhspOTjASxhXkFgaD-g3GN2v-HJ8cxhvOk86ffwQk-T5d0O44JcHHYTklBoCuSIQAvD_BwE.

happen to my husband when he went out with the kids. I try to really be aware of those fears. Once I realized some things about money, about how to be financially strong, I learned that I get to choose where to put it. They say money is a great servant, but a terrible master. I'm no longer afraid of not having enough, because I have a budget. I tell my money how to serve me and help me serve God.

Maybe you already understand how to budget money but haven't applied the same lesson to time. An important goal of self-care is that you feel in control. This goes back to fear. We are afraid because we are confused and our lives feel out of our control. What terrible thing might happen to us next if the world is out to get us and we have no say so in the matter?

That is not how God created us to function. He gave us all the tools we need to be productive and happy in this world, fallen as it is. He gave us the ability to focus our minds and make decisions about how we spend our resources. I've already talked about the resources of money and budgeting, but the same goes for time. Budgeting your time means you tell each minute of the day what is important. You will know how to spend your time based on what you value.

My List

For me, it starts with values. Before you can make a schedule (or a financial budget, for that matter) you must know what is important to *you*. I don't mean what is important to everyone else. Those things factor in, but what values and purposes has God given to you? Everything you do has a cost of time, so you don't want to squander your time on things that don't matter. Start with making a list of your highest priorities—the things you value most. In fact, do it here. If you are reading this as an e-book, then either make a note with the notes function on your e-reader or get out your journal.

If you don't know where to start, start with God and family, then go from there. On the bottom of the list should be the things you love to do for fun. Put those things on your list, but in their proper place.

Once you have made your list, you can look at your life and see where these things fit on your calendar and to-do lists.

Knowing what my values are, I make a list each night for the next day, first checking my calendar to make sure I know what appointments I have scheduled. I include everything I want to accomplish or that I need to do to stay organized. In this way I can feel in control. A lot of people get down on being in control, saying, "Don't be a control freak."

But I'm not talking about being a control freak. Control freaks try to change what cannot be changed. I'm talking about changing, or controlling, what *can* be changed. This is good stewardship of time. If you don't decide how you are going to spend your time, then others will decide for you. This passive and reactionary way of living is a one-way street toward mediocrity. Why not live an amazing life to the fullest?

The other effect of allowing others and disasters to be in control of your time is that you will become resentful—even with your husband! It is not just kids who will steal your time. Even if you don't have children, but you have a spouse, if you wake up at the same time as them and you don't have a list and a calendar, then they will set the tone and the agenda for you.

How are you spending your time? Does it look like your schedule has been made according to your values? If you value being successful at work, does your schedule show what you're doing to accomplish this? If you value spending quality time with your husband and kids, did it make the list? If not, you either don't value it, or you are still allowing someone else or cultural expectations to dictate your life. You are not in control.

You have not had the courage to change what can be changed.

Believe me, I am not casting the first stone, because I am not without fault in this area. But I am hoping to encourage you with the idea that it is entirely possible to list out your true values and then build your life around them. If you find that you do not have the possibility of controlling your time, then start thinking about your life and what you may need to do to reorganize it.

Make a list today of everything you are doing. How are you actually spending your time? You might be surprised. If you are thinking you don't want to know, that is a great sign you should do it today. Run to the truth and don't look back.

Chapter 8

To Love Yourself or Hate Yourself–Why Loving Yourself is Crucial and Right

"When you change your thoughts,
remember to also change your world."
–Norman Vincent Peale

Love for Humanity

IF YOU DON'T LOVE YOURSELF, you cannot love others. You only think you love others. But if you can't love yourself, it means you have a fundamental flaw in your thinking about humans. There is a reason Jesus said to "love your neighbor as yourself." He assumed we would love ourselves.

You were born to an imperfect woman. The majority of us were then raised by a version of her. She had good days and she had bad days. You started out with a fairly clean slate, although I do think we are all born with certain tendencies. Some parts of our personality seem to be genetic. However, much more importantly, most of how we are depends on how we are raised. As a baby, you looked at things and you perceived them without any understanding of what you were seeing.

The title of this chapter is "To Love Yourself or Hate Yourself—Why Loving Yourself is Crucial and Right." Let me ask you this: Do you want your child to hate themselves? If you said yes, we need to talk. My guess is that you said "no."

Why would our Father in heaven be any different?

Think about it this way: God made you an individual. You were created alone, saved (if you're saved) alone, and you will die and go to the Judgment alone. That means he created you as an entity. We talked about stewardship already but remember that the most basic unit of stewardship is your life. You must pursue life if you want to do anything else. You must seek to meet your needs for food, shelter, love, purpose, and self-actualization. You must do that. This requires love for yourself. It requires that you care about yourself. It does not require you to hate everyone else, but you must love yourself enough to take care of yourself (see Chapter 5 on self-care).

Think about that. Why am I using all of these words to convince you that not only is it okay to love yourself, but it is also a necessity? Remember, you cannot hate yourself and love others. Love is a value, and we value what we love. Let me go deep here: we cannot love another person or even a thing if we don't have values. We cannot have values, that is, things that we value, if we do not value ourselves. Why? Because if we don't value ourselves, why would we care that we value something or someone? To love someone is to say they are important to *me*. Why would it matter what is important to me if *I* don't matter?

If I love myself, I will give myself what *myself* wants, those things I value, those things I desire to gain and keep. I will give myself the people I value. I cannot value anyone if I don't value me, the *valuer*. I said I was going deep! Read all that again and think it over.

I'll recap: God loves you, and he wants you to love yourself, because he is a good Father, not a bad one.

You have to love yourself if you are going to love others, because to love others, you have to love humanity, God's crowning creation; his image-bearers. But you cannot say you love humanity and then not love yourself. You owe it to God and humanity to love yourself. Then you can obey Jesus when he says, "'Love others as well as you love yourself.' There is no other commandment that ranks with these." (Mark 12:30-31).

In the next chapter, we'll consider how to love our kids right in light of all this.

Chapter 9

How to Love Your Kids Right

"I am a strong woman because
a strong woman raised me."

I WANT MY GIRLS to say this about me. I feel this about my sons, as well. I teach them respect and how to treat a woman.

I loved my mom fiercely when I was a little girl. She made me her best friend. That put a lot of pressure on me because she wanted me to spend my time with her, even getting jealous if I had a good friend. As I got older, she didn't want me hanging out with friends if it meant I couldn't be with her.

I didn't like that, and I also didn't like that she wanted to talk to me about my boyfriends as though we were a couple of preteens gossiping together. I needed a mom. I didn't want her getting all excited, asking me all the details as though she was living vicariously through me, which she was.

I liked being able to tell her things, and I was always honest with her, but she took the news like a friend, not like the mom

I needed. There was a boundary line that was missing. I didn't need to hear about her feelings as though I was a mature woman who was her friend and not her young daughter. She didn't need to take me into her confidence about issues with my dad. When moms do that, they hurt their kids. The mind of a teen or preteen is not ready for those details. They barely know how to navigate life.

Moms who overshare with their children are being selfish. They are looking for some kind of emotional codependency to fill some void. They are looking for a way to feel young again by putting themselves on the same level as their daughter. It's abusive. My mom wanted to have a beer with me at fifteen, and I believe that is simply an insane and destructive way to parent. I know she did not do this maliciously. She herself was not parented properly. She married at sixteen and got stuck at that age—where she still is to this day.

It's hard to believe that some of those experiences actually happened because I could never dream of doing that with my own kids. You're not supposed to be that way. Parents are very precious, and they're supposed to be there for their child's whole life in a certain kind of role; to be respected and to give wisdom. They're not supposed to be your best friend. Kids will have plenty of friends throughout their lives, but we only have one mom and one dad.

That relationship should be honored by the mother, and the father should also hold his title with prestige and expect to be respected. Why?

At least part of the reason is that young children don't

yet know how to conceptualize. You can't tell a one-year-old, "honor God."

"Who's that," they will wonder?

A baby does know his mother and father. They are big people who provide, who discipline, who nurture and love them. As they grow, a child who respects her parents will be able to understand respect for God. If you love your children, insist that they respect you.

There is enormous pressure on parents. Many of us become parents when we're barely grown and have zero idea about how to do it! All we know is how we were raised. If we like how we were raised, we'll try to do it the same way. If we don't, we'll try to do the opposite. Either way, we've been trained by our parents. Even when we try to do the opposite, often our emotional training will kick in and we'll act like them, anyway.

We sometimes struggled with my oldest daughter, but she wasn't my friend. I wasn't going to talk to her about my marriage, my sex life, or our finances. That just wasn't my relationship with her. That's the stuff that I talked to my best friend about. If I was worried about how we were low on money, or Joe and I were having arguments, or something like that, the kids never knew about it. That would have hurt them and put us in a certain light in their minds that would not be good for them, at least before they were grown.

I hate that I haven't had that kind of mother since I was eleven. My mother has some great qualities, and I did get a lot of them from her. She's caring, a great homemaker, a great cook, and more. Unfortunately, I have not had a mother to respect, who I could look up to and be able to share things that I'm challenged with as a woman, a wife, and a mother and to have someone that's there that says, "I remember," and, "Let me tell you this one time back when your dad and I were having kids," and share some stories of wisdom.

That would be great.

I'm different with my own children. I've always wanted to be different, and I've achieved that so far. I have been the mother that I wanted to be to them, the mother I wish I'd had—mostly. We don't get a handbook, and we don't do everything right, but we learn to apologize when we need to and do better the next time.

When our children make bad choices, we love them anyway and we're always there. We don't condone, support, or approve of everything they do, but we're still there to always give love and support. That relationship gets messed up if you become their drinking buddy. It's just not good. There's something very special if a kid can revere her parents.

Let me offer a word here about respect. It is vitally important that we insist our kids respect us, but it is equally important that we do this dispassionately. Some parents are insecure and take disrespect so personally that they will borderline abuse their children for disrespecting them. That's not what I mean. God is not insecure when he calls us to honor and glorify him. He knows it is right for us to glorify him, because he is the most glorious being in existence. He wants us to give the most glory to the most glorious things. It's natural. It would be weird and dishonest if we didn't.

If a parent is insecure, then getting their children to respect them becomes a personal matter. They will teach their child to fear them, which they will until they are grown, at which point the kids will just hate them and rebel, at least behind their back.

Understanding Your Children

Everything I do with my kids is purposeful. I try to understand where they're coming from. They make mistakes sometimes because they are immature and don't know better. They get into something, maybe it's a dating relationship, and I tell them that I know that's got to be a super exciting feeling. It is not hard at all for me to feel vicariously excited watching them grow up and have these experiences. I remember being their age and what it was like, but then that other side as a mom says, "Just make sure that you watch out for this, and listen to God about that, and use wisdom here."

I'm always giving some advice on the tail end of whatever they're telling me. I can't help it, and I think that's how it's supposed to be.

My mom never gave me that kind of advice, but I needed it so much. I had other mom friends that were the same way. They were really close to their daughters, but they failed to guide the way for them. I've always wanted to provide that for my kids.

Therapy

This is as good of a place as any to make the case for therapy. Seriously, consider seeing a good counselor if you were raised on fallen planet Earth by fallen parents. I mean it. There is nothing more important than your emotional, mental, psychological, and spiritual health when it comes to your parenting.

I've known people who desperately wanted to be good parents. They went to parenting conferences, classes, and Bible studies. They read every book ever written on the subject, and they tried every technique they were taught. If there were ten steps to a new kid, five rules of raising children, or 100 days to a happy child, they were amazingly faithful about implementing them.

But these techniques didn't work. None of them. In fact, it seemed to make the children crazy. They'd see their mom reading a new book and start having PTSD about whatever "life change" was about to be imposed. Would it be less TV? More TV? Spanking, or no more spanking?

It didn't matter, because one thing never changed: the emotional health of the parents. The parents had not dealt with their own issues, and they lived on the energy created by fear and anxiety. They created unhealthy bonds with their kids, triangulation, and codependency. Techniques don't matter a bit if you aren't healthy enough to differentiate yourself from your family members. This is hard for a mother. She was one body with her babies at one point, and someone had to literally cut the cord between them. That right there is a metaphor that keeps on giving for life!

One of the greatest things I've heard from a therapist through the years is about life stages. According to this way of looking at life, there are four stages that we all progress through when it comes to our issues.

In stage one, you're going about what you were trained to do from childhood and doing whatever has been acceptable. You operate automatically and are *unconsciously dysfunctional.* Things aren't working for you. Your relationships don't work out, work isn't going well. You just aren't making it and are not happy.

Then, perhaps you start talking to someone wise, like a therapist or a pastor, and you move over into being *consciously dysfunctional.* Even though you still are not operating correctly or functionally, you're aware of it now. You are conscious that something isn't working.

Once you can identify what's not working, which thought patterns are harmful, which behaviors are leading to poor outcomes, or perhaps even why you engage in those behaviors, you can start to change. You start consciously doing things differently, not in a way that is yet natural for you, but in the way you understand to be correct. You take advice. You implement some guidance. You no longer act on unhealthy impulses, so your life is starting to change a bit. You are now in the stage of being *consciously functional.* You've made the changes, you're living better, your life's getting better, but it's taking a lot of thought. You have to really think before you speak or act. It's hard work but it pays off.

Then one day the magic happens. You wake up and you are *unconsciously functional.* Things are very good at this point, and you have overcome them! If you do not quit, this is what will happen. Suddenly, you are sailing through the areas in which you used to struggle. You probably have areas like that in your life. You can say, "Hey, I don't really struggle with that anymore."

The Stages of Living a Functional Life

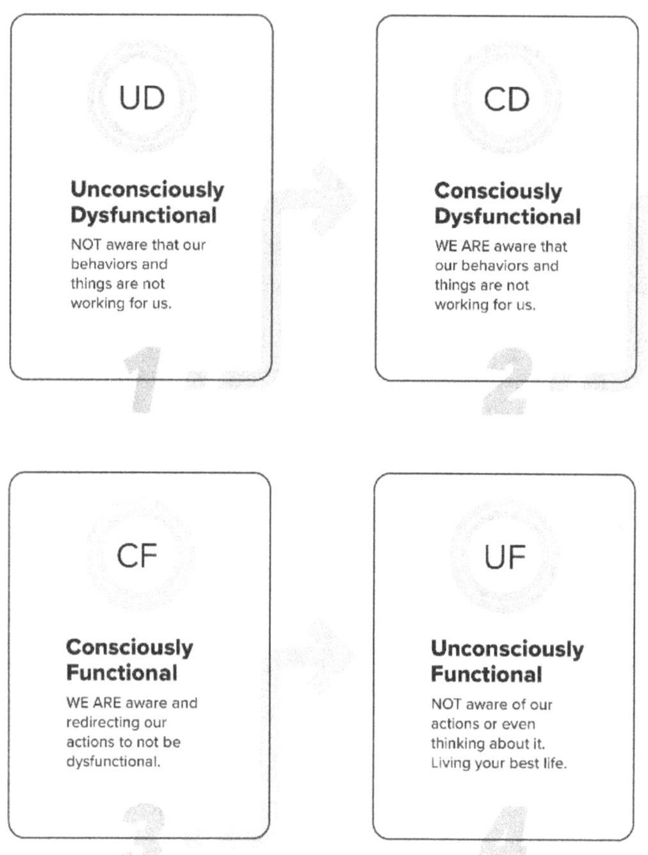

Many of these unhealthy behaviors changed without you trying too hard. Your environment changed and lent itself to a new way of living.

There are other things that you continue to struggle with, and you chalk up to the human condition, or you say, well, God has to change me and he hasn't yet. This goes back to courage and the serenity prayer. How will God change you? He'll give you the courage that you ask him for when you are ready to make a change.

The sad fact is most people don't understand this process. They want to change something, for instance, their eating habits. They say, "I'm going to stop eating sugar. The doctor says inflammation is killing me, and that sugar is one of the main sources of inflammation."

Simple, right? Don't eat sugar.

Ah, but it's not as easy as that. You like sugar. You love it, in fact. Your body chemistry responds to it in a big way. You crave it. In order to stop, you have to stay constantly vigilant. You have to be that weirdo who is constantly talking about it, or at least tempted to constantly talk about the dangers of sugar and inflammation. If you let your guard down, your body chemistry and emotions will take over. As soon as you are not focused, you won't have the necessary courage or motivation to change the habit. You'll give in, thinking, "Oh, I'll think about this later. Right now, I want what I want."

Maybe you don't want to give up sugar. Fine. You won't give it up until you have a reason to, but the reason is only the first step. Another step is deciding how to keep this in the front of your mind while you go about your day, which also requires you to be focused on work, kids, your spouse, and everything else that matters to you in your life.

"But I don't want to be obsessed about my diet," you might say.

That is perfectly understandable. I don't either, but there are only two ways to change your diet. The first way would be to move into the wilderness where you don't have access to those foods. Not going to do that? Then you must take the second way and be obsessed for a while. Why? Focus. The definition of focus is that it is singular.

How many resolutions do you have right now? Do yourself a favor and put them in order of importance. If you try to tackle all of them, you'll achieve none of them. Take them one at a time. This is how the mind works.

This is really good news, because first, it explains why you haven't been able to change. You simply haven't understood that the stage of conscious functionality is going to be long and hard. You felt bad about yourself when it was hard. You thought it was your fault.

It's not your fault! It's the way we're made.

We need to choose to focus, or we won't change.

Here are three steps and a promise:

Step One: Decide to focus

I believe that most people live without focus. They walk in the house and turn on the TV simply because the background noise takes away the need to focus. Focus is too painful. It's too confusing because many people haven't really thought about their lives. They haven't sorted out the fact that they are full of contradictions and are being pushed around by their feelings. They don't want to discover that they have pain to deal with and fears to face.

What would happen if you started to focus? You would have to deal with things. You might see you have some work to do. You might be able to see the direction of the path you're on, and the cliff you're about to walk off.

I believe you started reading this book because some part of you is seeking answers and change. You realize somewhere deep down you have a problem that has something to do with your mom, or that somehow originated there. You've likely made some internal discoveries as you've been reading. That is wonderful, but only if you decide to take action. Choose focus. Don't blank out your mind. Take a good hard look at yourself, your behavior, your feelings, and seek to understand what is going on. Ask God to help you. Have the courage to look. The courage to change starts there, with the courage to see. Before you can heed Paul's command to focus on good things, take a minute to see what you are focusing on now.

Even when you are trying to blank out, you know by now that thoughts creep into your mind continuously. Doubts, fears, and insecurities will follow you around. When you are out walking and realize someone is following you, you're supposed to turn around and confront them. This is the same response with intruding thoughts. Turn around and confront them. "Why are you following me? Where did you come from?" You ask, "Why do I think that?"

You know by now that I will say it *probably goes back to your mother.*

So, step one is to decide that living a life in focus is necessary. I cannot make a strong enough case for that. Living is seeing what *is* and *deciding* what it means and what to do about it. That is being human. That is being made in the image of God.

If you are not convinced, don't even read step two. Just skip to the next chapter or go back and start this one again. I mean it!

Step Two: Focus on a few particular things

What are you going to focus on? Feel free to list them here if you're reading the printed version of this book. If you're reading the e-book, you can use the "notes" feature to write things down.

____

____

____

____

____

____

____

____

____

____

____

____

____

After you have made a long list of things that are important to focus on, that is, the things that you value, then you must rank them so you can focus on each in turn.

Do that here:

____

____

____

____

____

____

____

____

____

____

____

____

____

Once you have these values ranked in order, take the one off the top and focus on it until you achieve the level of "unconsciously functional" in that area. It may take weeks, but the more you focus, the faster it will happen. When that happens, you'll likely be happier, assuming you ranked your values in an intelligent and *truthful* way.

For what it's worth, I learned this technique from an intensive therapy book that I got from Dr. John Friel's Clear

Life Clinic. He does not do one-hour solo therapy sessions. Early on, my husband and I struggled in our marriage. Joe was complaining that I had not yet put any boundaries on my relationship with my parents and their involvement in our life. I had gone to see a traditional therapist, and she said, "You need intensive therapy."

So, she told me about Dr. Friel, and I flew to where he was to take part in three days, eight hours each day, of intensive group therapy. I loved it, and it changed my life. Why did that work? Because it forced me to spend three solid days focusing and obsessing on one problem. Do you want to change? You don't necessarily have to go to an intensive clinic, but you must focus your mind on what you want to change. Rank the things you want to change in order of importance. Start with the most urgent item and then focus on it.

Step Three: Put into practice what you've written down

Focus on the things you want to change, and then practice those things. That is the way to be transformed.

Now, What Does This Have to Do with Parenting?

This is a chapter on how to love your kids properly. My point is this: you must be healthy in order to love your kids well. You must know who you are, and it helps to be following God.

We were discussing how not to become your mother, and how not to make the opposite mistake by becoming the opposite of your mother, doing things just because it is not what your mother did. We're talking about being the kind of healthy follower of Jesus who can raise kids from a place of wisdom, understanding their role as a parent. You're not a friend, but a mom.

If my own mother had gone through some good therapy, she could have realized that the hole in her heart that caused her to cheat on my dad could have been filled by God. She could have learned that she could not fill the hole with affection and friendship from her daughter, either. She could have had the courage to be the mom I needed, to live the life she had been called to, and do what's right.

Focus on God and what is right. Make sure you have a healthy identity rooted in Christ, and then ask God to teach you how to be a good and conscientious mother. He will show you. If you focus intensely on this, God will change you, which will change your parenting and change your kids. You will love your children rightly and show them God by how you treat them.

Chapter 10

Choose to Have a Good Relationship or No Relationship by Setting Boundaries

"Do what you feel in your heart to be right—
for you'll be criticized anyway."
–Eleanor Roosevelt

PERHAPS YOU'VE HEARD of the book *Boundaries* by Henry Cloud and John Townsend. It is an important book for anyone who has a tendency toward codependent relationships. Creating boundaries is a crucial concept, but many people fear that it is unloving to create boundaries. According to the authors:

The owner of the property is legally responsible for what happens on his or her property. Nonowners are not responsible for the property.

Physical boundaries mark a visible property line that someone holds the deed to. You can go to the county courthouse and find out exactly where those boundaries of responsibility are and whom to call if you have business there.

In the spiritual world, boundaries are just as real, but often harder to see. Boundaries define us. They define what is me and what is not me. A boundary shows me where I end and someone else begins, leading me to a sense of ownership...

Knowing what I am to take ownership of and taking responsibility for those things gives me freedom. If I know where my yard begins and ends, I am free to do with it what I like. Taking responsibility for my life opens up many different options. However, if I do not "own" my life, my choices and options become very limited.

Boundaries show the important distinction between who I am responsible for, which is me, and who I am only responsible to, which is everyone else.

Another psychologist, Alfred Adler, lived at the time of Sigmund Freud and Carl Jung, and at the time was considered as important as those two giants. Unlike Freud and Jung, Adler's ideas were so commonsensical that his own name has practically faded away as his concepts have become so universally accepted. He used the phrase "the separation of tasks" to talk about the same concept.

According to Adler, we all have our own tasks in life. Being human is to be one who has responsibility for their life. The Bible calls it stewardship. You have things you are responsible for, and I have things I am responsible for. If I try to take over your responsibilities, I am violating your will and conscience. If I try to make you do something by manipulating or enslaving you in some way, I violate you. If I let you take responsibility for my tasks or cross my boundary lines, I allow you to violate me.

When we do that, we hurt people. We create codependent relationships. For example, if my mother decides today that she wants to go run off with another man again, she will also want me to approve. I know this from experience. She will simultaneously ignore me for a while as she is wrapped up in the relationship, thinking it is the best thing that ever happened to her, and that this guy is her "soul mate."

My task, my "property," would be to tell her, "Mom, this is crazy, you shouldn't do that to your husband."

It's not that it is none of my business. It is only that my responsibility *to* my mom and *to* her husband is to speak the truth. The Bible tells us to speak the truth in love: "God wants us to grow up, to know the whole truth and tell it in love—like Christ in everything" (Eph 4:15).

I might not feel like doing that, but I need to do it.

Her task is to hear what I'm saying and consider it. If she listens and says, "Oh, Sabrina, you're right," then that is great.

It is her task to either break up with the guy, and go back to her husband, or it is also her task to ignore me and go off and wreck her life. The operative word is "her" life. It's not my life.

How does this usually go down? Usually, I cross her boundaries. I try to stop her. I feel responsible, so I end up taking responsibility for her choices. I learned to do that as a little girl. It is almost as though it feels irresponsible not to.

Consider that it violates someone's boundaries, their property, and their task, to take on the responsibility of making someone else happy. They may very well want you to. They may be inviting you every day to come onto their property and fix whatever is making them unhappy. But don't do it.

When I cross my mother's boundary lines, or I let her cross mine, I get incredibly resentful. Do you have someone in your life who you find yourself being rude to all the time? Do you catch yourself looking for little ways to hurt them? My husband says I speak harshly to my parents at times. It's true, and the reason is that we have blurred boundary lines. I resent them because I don't set a clear enough boundary. Resentment gets in the way of real love.

But what if I didn't take responsibility for my mother's life? What if I encouraged her, called her out, and then just loved her? What if I didn't feel the need to jump over onto her "property" and fix everything? Could you do that with your own mother? Could you do that with your kids?

You likely need permission to hold your relationships with an open hand. This applies to people you are supposed to be leading, as well. You cannot lead people by violating their will. You can only show them the truth and leave their response up to them.

What You Need is Permission

If you are the kind of person who tends to take on responsibility, then you probably feel guilty when you realize that you could fix something, but you're not doing it. You feel anxious. You know what to do and may even see a way to make it happen. So, you feel irresponsible if you don't fix it, or at least if you don't spend a bunch of time and energy worrying about it. Let me give you permission to stay on your own property.

Trust me, it is the best way. It is the most loving way. In fact, we hurt people when we take away their agency. We hurt them when we don't allow them to face the consequences that could cause them to actually change.

Can you be honest with yourself about something? Do you take pride and a sense of superiority in being the "go-to" gal who can take care of everybody else? Does it hurt your pride when those you see yourself responsible for are not doing well? Permission not to worry about what others are doing comes when you understand *stewardship*.

Stewardship

God has given each person one talent, two talents, three talents, or more. He's given the time, energy, and skill for everyone to make the most of their life. God has assigned things to them to steward, to manage, for him. He will demand an account. What they are going through in their life is their task, not yours. You don't just have permission to back off, but a command to do so. "Each of you must take responsibility for doing the creative best you can with your own life" (Gal 6:5).

This is the way God created us. Anything less than taking responsibility for our own lives is less than human. Don't help someone shirk their responsibility. Don't enable someone. That's not what you're called to do.

You have your own responsibilities, and one of them is not dominating people (yes, when you try to take responsibility for someone else's actions, you dominate them). When God created us and said, "subdue the earth," he meant the earth, not other people. When he said to have dominion over the animals, that did not include each other. Each man and woman are responsible for their own life. Entrust your people to God. Worry about them only long enough to pray for them and tell them the truth. Cast your burden on Christ.

As you cast the burden on Jesus, he will set for you an example of how to lead people, because he will do what he did when he walked the Earth as a human. He will tell the truth, walk his own straight path, and *invite* others to follow him. He will not force anyone to follow. If anybody could use force, it is Jesus. If anyone should, it is Jesus. But he won't because he made us to be humans, not robots, not even animals. We have to bear the responsibility of our humanity and let others do the same, even when we love them and don't want to watch them fail. Receive permission to let God be God and walk your own path in peace.

A Good Relationship or No Relationship

You can have a good relationship if you are willing to have no other kind. This sounds harsh, and it sounds untrue because you likely have relationships that are somewhere in the middle. You might even call them good relationships, but unless there are no compromises when it comes to boundaries, then you don't truly have a good relationship. You have accepted some things that are allowing unhappiness to settle on you.

If you're not sure if this is true, answer this question: Do you feel resentment? If you feel *any* resentment, then you are compromising and violating each other's boundaries, taking each other's tasks.

Another question for you to consider is: Are you harsh with the person? If so, it is because you are angry at them on some level. You don't want to deal with what makes you angry and resentful, but you do want to get back at them.

We do this with our kids all the time. Parents who don't discipline their kids will always find little ways to hurt them. Is that shocking? Think about it. Most of your own wounds were caused by a parent who didn't know how to parent you and felt resentment towards you, life, and God, and took it out on you in a thousand microaggressions. It wasn't your fault. They just didn't quite know what they were doing.

My friend watched his mother-in-law speaking abusively to her own ninety-year-old mother. It seemed like every time he heard them interacting, she was speaking harshly to her mom and her tone was that her mother was stupid and trying her patience. According to my friend, the ninety-year-old mother was sweet and easy to please, undemanding in her old age. So, he asked his mother-in-law one day if she noticed that she was always irritable with her mother. She seemed a little ashamed of herself but said she couldn't help it. When he asked if her mother had done anything to upset her growing up that hadn't been dealt with, out came a flood of stories with great emotion. My friend thought, "Aha, this can be solved," and suggested she have a talk with her mom, and then forgive her.

She refused, saying, "I could never do that."

This is so sad. The old woman died with the issues

unresolved. My friend's own wife, the daughter of the mother-in-law and adoring granddaughter of the old mother, could see that she was following the same pattern. She decided not to live the same way and confronted her mother about some things in her childhood that were still causing her pain. Then she forgave her mom. The resentment she'd felt toward her own mother was gone. What seemed to be a generational curse was broken forever.

Want to hear the most interesting part? My friend's wife's mom did not really understand, and her apology was half-hearted. It didn't matter to my friend's wife. She had been able to say her piece. This is step one to setting those clear boundaries so that you can have a great relationship or no relationship. She has a great relationship with her mother now because property lines are clear and there is *individuation,* meaning each gets their autonomy as individuals, and nothing ever happens that leaves resentment. If any conflict arises, it is dealt with in a straightforward, honest manner.

Death to Self

One of the most mysterious and misapplied concepts in the Christian faith is death to self. Jesus said we must take up our cross and follow him in his death. He said if we would find our life, we must lose it. What on Earth, or in heaven, does this mean?

Of all that it could mean, one thing I know is that dying to self is what has to happen for healthy confrontation and assertive conflict resolution. It is *fear* that must die; your fearful self. If you want to know how to die to self, beyond the original death of giving your life to Christ, this is it: Face your fears. Do the uncomfortable. Let resentment die. Be assertive. The old unassertive self must go for you to be truly happy and have good relationships. Don't settle for anything else.

Imagine what your life would be like if your mother, your kids, or your husband simply could not hurt you, or at least not mortally wound you, because you were able to hold your property lines without getting upset. You can simply lay down the law, saying, "Here are my boundaries."

Your boundaries may have to do with what the other person can say to you and not say to you. You might not want them to lie to you anymore. You could say, "If you lie to me, we will not talk."

"But I am afraid."

You must love God, truth, righteousness, and justice enough to say, "Better to be alone than with people who hurt me, pull me down, or make me compromise my values."

If you put boundaries in place and hold to them, it will be brutally difficult *at first*, but then it will be amazing. Two wonderful, miraculous things will happen. One, you will become a different, more integrated, more courageous person, and two, you will either have a good relationship with your mother, or you will not have to worry about her in your life.

Think about the things that bring you resentment toward your mother, father, or anyone else, and determine not to allow those things to take place. Be courageous, and you and your relationships will be transformed!

Chapter 11

Their Marriage, My Marriage, Your Marriage—The Good, the Bad, and the Ugly

> "Successful mothers are not the ones that
> never struggled. They are the ones that
> never give up despite the struggles."
> –Sharon Jaynes

ONE OF THE MOST PROMINENT themes in this book is how your life reflects the way you were raised, especially those aspects of life that you learned directly from your mother. I can think of two things that stand out as the most difficult to overcome. One is money and how you think of it and handle it. That's for another book. The other is marriage.

As a little girl, my parents, in spite of everything that happened later, modeled what still feels to me today like a perfect marriage and family. Marriage was honored. In spite of the fact that I was close with my parents, and my mom especially even though she treated me like a friend sometimes, they truly modeled a good marriage. Mom and Dad did things that they kept just between the two of them.

I saw that marriage was a strong commitment, especially as it related to sex. My dad always talked to me about it and warned me, saying, "If you're going on a date, put a penny between your knees for birth control."

Because, of course, if you don't spread your legs, you won't have sex. Don't let the penny fall to the ground! He also was probably the one to coin the well-known phrase, "Why buy the cow when you can get the milk for free?"

It was entrenched in me that men will sleep with girls, but they will marry a virgin, so keep yourself pure for the wedding night.

Interestingly, that is not how my parents did it. They got married very young because my mom was pregnant with me. My dad slept with a lot of girls in high school. That is what often happens when parents feel they messed up. They want to make sure their kids don't make the same mistakes they did, so this was a constant theme.

But up until it wasn't good, it was great—to me, perfect. My dad worked very hard to provide for us and did whatever he had to do to pay the bills. My mom took care of me, the house, and my dad. She stayed home, and she cooked and cleaned so we could have a good home. She would do my hair every day, putting it in pigtails, then she'd get the laundry done and start fixing homemade spaghetti sauce at lunchtime so it could be ready for dinner. Or she might peel potatoes or string green beans. Whatever food it was, it was a lot of work and tasted good.

My mom packed my dad's lunch every day and got up to see him off to work. Then she would be the homeroom mom at kindergarten, helping with Christmas parties and various other things. That's just what she did.

My dad was and is very loyal. He said that he knew at a young age that he wanted to be a family man and work and have a home. He always loved coming home, and he took a lot of pride in his house. He kept it up on the outside. When he was off work, he built decks, poured extra concrete for sidewalks, and he took a lot of pride in keeping his vehicles washed, whether they were new or old. Whatever was his, he took pride in. After sixteen hours of working, he loved to come home and be with us. That's just the way he was.

I saw that my mom and dad were very much in love for the first ten years of my life, and I loved it. I took nothing but positive memories from those days, and they have truly shaped the way I live my own family life.

My Own Lapse in Faithfulness

Before I go on to how things changed after that, I want to say that I have tried to model my own life on what I saw in those first ten years, but I have to take this moment to show how I took a step or two down the path of infidelity. I'm telling you now because we overcame it.

When I was twenty-five, Tristan was born and Joe and I made the decision that I would quit my job and stay home with the baby. I hated the thought of him going to daycare. I still dreamed of creating for my kids what I had for the first ten years of my life, but when Tristan was three, my friend told me the place where she worked could use some help if I wanted a part-time job. Tristan and I were very close, and since he was a little too clingy, it seemed like a good idea to give him some time without me. Up to that point, whenever I was out of sight, he'd cry miserably.

Joe and I decided that he could go to the preschool at the Methodist Church, and I would take the job. It was only two hours a day, two days a week, and seemed like a good plan. Tuesdays and Thursdays I would file paperwork. Others would spend the day pulling out files in the course of whatever they did, and then I'd come in and put them all back again.

This was a fun place to work, because the owner, a twenty-two-year-old who had finished school and inherited a business, was a lot of laughs. We all got along very well, and I enjoyed the social interaction. Add to this the fact that Joe was working close to 100 hours most weeks and we were building our first home. Joe and I had grown disconnected from each other, creating a recipe for something not good. When you start spending your emotional energy on everyone but your spouse, things can easily get sideways.

Though I wasn't anything but friends with the owner, it felt a little exciting that he would flirt with me, and I returned the gesture. What could it hurt? Without attention at home, I didn't realize how much I was craving this. I did feel slightly guilty, but then, we weren't doing anything but flirting . . . at first.

Three or four months into the job, it progressed to us talking on the phone on the days I was off. No big deal, right? It was fun to talk and laugh. It was just an innocent connection with somebody. He was also married, and there wasn't a lot of communication going on there, so we were able to discuss it together. We knew we both loved our spouses, but our friendship was becoming more and more important to us. We discussed the fact that this was simply a good friendship, and it could go no further than that. We would be close friends and nothing more. We would share an emotional connection, supporting each other, and maybe we could help each other have better marriages.

Unfortunately, there is something about friendships between men and women

that never stay that way. We were simply friends. Simply connected emotionally and that was it, until it progressed, and one day we found ourselves kissing at work. This was scary and also exciting, sadly.

Thank God this foolishness did not progress beyond kissing, but we were kidding ourselves thinking it was somehow okay. We sure weren't telling our spouses about it. That should have been a clue, but when you don't want to see something . . .

Eventually, our consciences caught up with us. We faced facts and knew we were wrong to be doing that. I quit working there, and though at first, we thought we could just stay friends, we eventually stopped talking altogether. I felt so guilty.

One day when I was with Joe, my phone rang. It was him! "Called to say hi and see how you are doing," he said.

My face turned red and I said, "You must have the wrong number."

I told Joe immediately who had called and what had happened. It was such a relief to come clean, but at the same time, my heart sank in fear that Joe would leave me. Joe and I talked about it, and he said, "I know that you are a wonderful person. I know that this isn't the type of person that you are. That's why I will stay with you. I know I was working all the time. I know that. The circumstances were perfect for something like that to happen."

I'm thankful that when it all came out, it had already ended. Even with all those things factored in, Joe wanted to keep moving forward with the marriage. I'm so thankful that he did because now we've been together for almost thirty wonderful years!

Of course, Joe did end up talking to the guy, and he said, "Never call her again."

He said, "You tell your wife about it, or I'm going to call and tell her. It's not that I hate you, but she deserves to know, too."

So, he told his wife, and I meant to call her the next week. Actually, it was funny because we were living with mom and dad at the time this was going on—we were building a house right next door to them. I remember telling mom everything that was going on, and I asked her if she'd please call this woman for me, because I was afraid she wouldn't speak to me. I said, "Please call her and tell her that I'm so sorry, that I'm just so sorry that I hurt her, that I don't know what happened or why I did that, and I just truly apologize."

I thought she'd never forgive me, but I remember how nice she was. She was raised as very good Christian girl in a strong, well-known family from the area. She told Mom, "It'll be hard for me to forget; actually, I'll never forget, but I do forgive her. Tell her I forgive her."

I was so touched by that, that she was so mature, and in the way that she forgave me. She was younger than me, but she'd had a much better life than I had growing up.

Anyway, it was over at that point, and I never spoke to him again until years later when, by some weird coincidence, we ended up doing some business with him. I mean, I'd see him every once in a while, because our kids grew up in the same town, but we never interacted.

I did have tremendous guilt. I had to work through a lot of it. I had to pray to God a lot, specifically asking when I could ever feel like I wasn't a bad person again. It took several years for me to not feel guilty and to really *feel* like I had received forgiveness. After many years, I finally feel okay about it. I say I feel okay about it, but I'm still not glad it happened. I'd never be proud that it happened, but it did and there is nothing I can do to change it, so I have accepted it. To err is human, after all. It's what you do next that defines you and your character.

I'm relieved that something like that happened, yet I didn't let it define me for the rest of my life. It made me realize that you better watch what you are thinking and doing. I didn't think something like that would ever happen to me, but it taught me how anyone can slip up and can get into trouble. From that point forward, I was always very careful. I'm a friendly person, and I don't have a problem being friends with guys or girls. Now I'm just always cautious, and if I feel like anything's getting to where they get the wrong idea from me, or from the comments made, then I just stop. I reverse immediately and get myself out of that situation and put distance between me and that person. I know now how not to get myself in that situation again.

I'm including this chapter because I don't want it to seem like I'm so perfect and never make mistakes. I also know that many people think they are bound to make the same mistakes as their parents, and while it looked for a minute like I was on the same path, by God's grace and Joe's forgiveness, I was able to turn from it. I know you have probably done some things you feel ashamed of that threaten to define you, but they don't define you, especially if you have given your life to God and turned from those old ways. You can recover and you can feel like the new person you are in time.

I realized I'm not perfect through that experience. I realized I make mistakes, but we will all make mistakes. I have mistakes behind me, and I no doubt have some ahead of me to make, but it's about whether we let them ruin our life or make the necessary changes. Instead, we have to take them in and say, "Listen, oh my gosh, I can't believe this happened to me, I can't believe it. I allowed this to happen. I didn't have my guard up, or I didn't see this coming."

We are able to recognize these things and then change the course.

This also applies to the things we say. My mouth just runs sometimes, and I say things harsher than I mean to. Now, thankfully, I'm mature and I've learned. If I say something that's sharp, I don't just wait and let that go for two days. I stop immediately and say, "Hold on, let me say I'm sorry. I didn't mean for that to come out that way. I've had a hard day and I shouldn't have taken it out on you."

I change the direction of the conversation, and that, I think, is what we can do with the small things like that.

It works for the big things, too. I could have ruined my marriage, but I think because I recognized and stopped it, we were able to save our marriage. I could have kept going and said, "Oh, well, you know, I've already gone this far. So, it's over, it's ruined. Why not? Who cares?"

It's never too late to stop any time you feel like you're going down the wrong road and fight for what you know is right for yourself, for your husband, and for your family. If you have gone down a bad path, you can always stop and start over.

Practical Tips for a Better Marriage

Good marriages don't get good by accident. It takes intentionality. There is more than one decent way to run a household faithfully, and some of it depends on both spouses and their personalities. But here are some fairly universal principles into which I could distill my philosophy of marriage:

Be best friends with your spouse.

It's not that you shouldn't have girlfriends and he shouldn't have guy friends. It's healthy to have friends to do some things with, but we had married friends who would take it too far. They had girls' nights out and they would go to bars and clubs and party like they were single. Joe and I never did that. We went out, but we went together. We would also have friends over for drinks and cookouts.

We love to sit on the porch together and talk. The kids know that when we're out there like that, we're on a little date, and when we're done connecting we'll spend time with them.

Figure out how to take care of your household.

When the kids were little, Joe worked hard and I stayed home with the kids. I know not everyone wants to do that, but if you don't manage your kids and household, things will fall apart quickly. Having loved my own family experience when my mom stayed home, I knew that's what I wanted to do. There were times when I felt like I needed to work. The financial needs were too great, and I felt like we could get ahead if I worked. I was a nurse off and on and worked when I needed to. Then I would feel like I needed to get focused on the kids and I'd go full-time at home again for a year or two.

The reality is that my priority was always the home. Even when I worked, I made sure I knew how the house was going to get clean, the kids would be taken care of, and the family would be fed. Because my friends weren't raised this way, they didn't really understand it. I liked to take care of Joe and the household. That's what I saw my mom do in the good years and I loved it. I enjoyed it.

Joe would go off to work, and I'd clean. I'd take the kids to the park then go for a stroll. Then we'd come back and have lunch, they'd take a nap, and everything was very scheduled.

After naptime we'd go pick up their older sister from school. There was laundry to wash, food to cook, and when Joe came home from working seven days a week, I'd have his food ready for him. I'd pack his lunch and lay out his clean clothes. My friends would say, "Why are you doing all this?"

But he was working hard. I loved him, and I loved taking care of him. I still get a lot of joy out of it.

If that is not what you want to do, I'd suggest you at least need to cultivate a spirit of care for your home and family. Don't get me wrong. Don't hear me say that I couldn't do what I wanted. I did what I wanted. Don't hear me say that Joe never helped around the house. He did all the time, especially when we decided that I was going to work. He took more of the load, but I always took it upon myself to make sure the systems were in place for our household and our kids.

Most recently, we felt called to start a new health business in West Palm Beach, which meant I'm traveling there a lot. Our kids are a little older now, but they're still at home, and I have to make sure everything is taken care of, only now we hire help. I'm by no means hands off, but we knew this would be a hustle year, getting something off the ground, and we'd need some help. I'm out of town three days a week, but Joe picks up the slack. We discussed it, and we are solid enough to do it. Our housekeeper/nanny helps a ton every day, working in the middle of the day while neither one of us is at home.

I know that if it came down to keeping up the home or me working, I'd quit working, because Joe and I both have standards about how our home is run. It's important.

Talk and dream together.

Joe and I spend a good deal of time dreaming about what's next in our lives. We love to set goals and visualize five, ten, twenty years down the road. What do we want to be doing? Where do we want to be? How are we going to get there?

I remember when we were young and didn't have very much money, even when we were dating, we'd take boat rides on his dad's little bass boat. We'd see the big houses on the water and dream. "Wow. What did that person do to own that house?"

It seemed a long way off from where we were, but we learned to dream together and became big visionaries, willing to dream and then work hard to get the things we knew we wanted for our family. We still live that way today. Even at our age, we still foresee some great things we want to do together in the next five, ten, and fifteen years.

Prioritize your marriage, even over the kids.

Please hear me out on this point. Kids are extremely important, in that I suppose you can divorce your spouse if it comes to extremes, but you can't divorce your kids. That said, if you don't prioritize your marriage, you will grow distant, resentments will build into problems, and then one of two things will occur: You'll exist in a loveless marriage, or you'll divorce. Neither one is fun nor necessary.

Some people teach that the love you had when you first got together fades into something else. Romantic feelings "grow" into a less romantic *agape* sort of love. Don't buy it. It's true that when you first get together there are all sorts of hormonal forces at play causing you to be easily sexually attracted to each other. It's true those feelings give way as your relationship is no longer novel. But you can absolutely cultivate romantic feelings with a little bit of intentionality and creativity.

Teach the kids about Mom and Dad time. Show them there are times not to interrupt you. When he or both of you get home from work in the evening, set aside the first few minutes to be alone and connect. Make sure the kids know that this is a time they are not to interrupt you unless there is an emergency.

Certain nights of the week, I'd get the kids fed and get them watching a movie, and we'd say, "Now listen, you're going to stay inside and watch TV while we sit on the back porch and talk and have a little date."

There are times they know they can all camp out in our room, and there are times they know they can't.

They know their father and I take weekend trips without them sometimes. We hug and kiss each other in the kitchen. "Ooh, gross, stop!"

We talk about how much we love each other, and, if asked, they would definitely say, "Our mom and dad love each other!"

Insist the kids respect you and your husband.

Respect is a big deal in our household. No tone, no attitude, no back talk, no "sassing." This is how I was raised. I think I may have already said this, but God calls us in the Ten Commandments to honor our father and mother. He promises we'll "live long in the land" if we do. The reason is that a person who respects and honors their parents will respect and honor their Father in heaven, which is of ultra-importance. Respect is big in our household. We value love as well, but respect is number one.

Respect each other.

We have a fun bit of sarcasm that goes on, a little bit of joking, but never to the point of disrespect, so we have a great relationship.

Be unified with your spouse.

Don't undermine one another to the kids. Back each other up. The fact is, unless one of you is a pushover, you're going to have disagreements, especially about how to raise the kids. You must present a unified front and respect each other in front of the kids. If one of you disrespects the other, the kids will pick up on it and disrespect that spouse. This is not good.

I tend to discipline the kids a bit more than Joe. Even if he doesn't agree, he doesn't say anything other than, "Listen to your mother."

Then he might tell me later, "Hey, you were a little bit tough on the boys." But sometimes he'll actually say, "You know, you really caught the boys on that and I hope you felt that I had your back."

Be unified.

Choose your battles.

I've learned through the years that every marriage that makes it is one in which the husband and wife choose their battles. Some things are worth a good and healthy conflict, but sometimes you need to just be quiet and bear with one another. Joe is a procrastinator. I am anything but. I don't like to do anything today that I can do yesterday! Recently there were some boxes in the garage. I said, "Joe, we have some company coming over tomorrow; I'd like you to move these boxes over to the other garage."

He said, "Oh no, that's okay. I'm going to the office in the morning. I'm going to take them then."

I was thinking in my head, "No you won't. You won't take the boxes in the morning. You'll run late like you always run late, and you won't take them. I'll end up having to move them myself."

But I didn't say that. I said, "Okay, please don't forget, because I really want them out."

He said, "Oh no, I won't."

Well, he forgot. He often forgets in those situations. I know he's not lazy, because he works incredibly hard to provide for us. But he comes by procrastination naturally. The point is, in the past I would have called him and said, "Why did you forget to take the boxes? I had to move them myself!"

That would really get me in a bad mood, taking it personally. But now, I just move them myself and let it go. I have a great husband and a great relationship with him. I have accepted how he is. If the worst thing about my marriage is that I have to move some boxes, I'll take that. I have evolved to being more lighthearted and not nitpick him to death. I used to do that, and it hurt our marriage and did nothing to help his procrastination. Let God worry about changing your husband. If you will love him as he is, you'll have a better marriage.

I learned most of these principles from the first ten years of my parents' marriage. As I said before, it was a dream. I loved every minute of it, and I think of it as perfect, even though it probably wasn't.

Then things shifted. When my mom started leaving and going off to be with other men, of course, everything changed. For years I was confused about my dad's role in this. He took care of us so well, but at times he became very controlling. He never wanted her to get a job. He liked her to stay home. I thought maybe this was overbearing and stifling and that it pushed her away.

I've realized over the years that wasn't really what happened because my mom has never been able to stay with any kind of man since. For a long time, my dad would wait for her to come back, and when she did, he'd accept her, hopeful that this time she'd settle down and stay. But she never did, and eventually he remarried and became just as faithful to his current wife, Joe's mother. He's a one-woman man, and I guess I got most of my values about what a marriage should be from him.

I should remind the reader that I was married the first time very young, and I'm sure that the issues with my parents had a big part to play in my getting married in the first place, and the marriage not working out, because I was divorced by the time my daughter was born. But I've been married to Joe for nearly thirty years, and it's wonderful.

No matter how you were raised, take the good you saw in your parents and emulate it. Take the not-so-good and figure out what was wrong and why it was wrong and make the changes you need to. Look for those things in yourself and work on them. God will help you.

In my case, it simply comes down to trusting that every once in a while, you might not feel like you did when you were first dating your husband. What was going on with my mom? Well, I would not want to say that I can understand her completely, but I could take a pretty educated guess and learn some lessons from her mistakes.

First, she did not have a marriage grounded in faith, therefore it was not grounded in faithfulness. Sometimes, we just need to look to God and see that he says to be faithful for life to our spouse, and to keep vows until death do us part. I'm not saying there are never circumstances that could warrant a divorce, but just getting bored or falling out of love are not those circumstances.

I've learned from my mother that I might sometimes feel empty and need excitement. Unfortunately, for my mom, the answer is found in an ungodly rotation of men. I've learned from watching her closely, however, that a new man doesn't satisfy her. My mother has reinforced this behavior in herself by engaging in it over and over again so that she is utterly predictable on this point. She will feel empty. Her sinful nature will tell her all she needs is to get a new man to fall in love with her; that even in her old age, she's still got it. If she's still got it, she's still worthy, she's still worth something. This is almost too tragic to write.

How many of us do this at least on some level, even if it is less destructive than my mother's actions? We feel empty, then try to fill the void with what our brain tells us will fill it. *Only God can fill it,* and only living according to his way for us in the world can actually fill the emptiness and leave us satisfied. I feel sorry for my mom, and I pray for her constantly to find Jesus. It's so painfully obvious to me that that is what she longs for. If you want to have a good marriage, put your husband second. Put Jesus first.

Chapter 12

Being a Yaya—It's a Blessing and a Curse!

"A grandmother thinks of her grandchildren day and night, even when they are not with her. She will always love them more than anyone would understand."
–Karen Gibbs

NOW I WANT TO SAY SOMETHING about being a grandmother, or in my case, a Yaya. There is a whole lot of happiness and pain that goes with that role.

I have realized that when you are young and raising kids, you think that you're going to get through all the hard parts, and then your kids will turn eighteen and go off to college, or get a job, and take care of themselves, and you will worry less.

In my experience, it's worse when they move outside of your home.

There is a peace that you can't understand until your kids are no longer under your roof. I still have "the littles," my younger children, here at home, and knowing that I have my hand of protection over them, and I have at least *some* control over their lives, feels very safe going to bed at night. I know that they're okay, and that's all a mother wants most of the time.

But when your kids grow up and they move out, you don't know that they're okay, and you worry about them terribly. Even if they're doing well, you still worry about them and miss them. The mother in us doesn't want to stop tucking them in at night. Sometimes when I go to bed, I text the older kids. My empty nest got filled with younger children, but there is still an empty space for the older ones. They go through things. They have job losses, they get sick, and they go through a divorce. They have sad things happen like miscarriages. You just want to be there to hold them and to fix everything. But you don't live together, which makes a big difference, and they don't obey you anymore, even when you still think you know what's best for them.

I am challenged today as a mother because as I raised my kids, I was very close with my own parents. I am learning all the time how that has affected the way I think things should be now, and I want to make sure to maintain a good relationship with my adult children.

When your children grow up and find the loves of their lives, it changes your own life. I hadn't thought much about that because I stayed so close to my own parents. My daughter got married and moved out of town. I wasn't ready for that, because that isn't what I did. I had always imagined it would be with my kids like it was for me with my parents. I want that.

I want them to be close, and I want to still be in their lives.

She doesn't live more than an hour away, but that's farther away than I ever dreamed would be the case. It just didn't occur to me. I planned on her kids being able to come over for lunch. I imagined I'd go to pick up the grandkids from their school often. But they live an hour away from my house. And coming to terms with that has been difficult and sad.

My grown son married, and he and his wife are more loners. He works a lot and doesn't get together with family much when he's home. They all come over for holidays and things, but I have to accept that they have their own lives, and they don't yet know how time flies and how important it is to spend time with the older members of the family because they could be gone before they know it.

I cry a lot over all this, because I miss seeing my son and my daughter and their kids, but they have their own lives, and I know their spouses don't want to see me at their house all the time. The distance is painful, but you have to take a deep breath and realize they have to leave the nest and do their own thing.

Being Yaya

My grandchildren call me Yaya, and I love it.

I think that I am like all the other grandmothers out there. When I have the grandkids, I want to teach them things; I want to leave a mark on their lives. I want to teach my granddaughters how to cook and respect themselves and others, and I want to teach my grandsons how to be respectful, hardworking, and kind. I want to teach them all the old school values.

It's something that is very important, and I think it helps to shape grandkids. Every family is different regarding how much time they spend with the grandparents, but most of us Yayas, and Nanas, and Grammas, and Mamaws, and Mimis—we wish we could have more time. I've cried many tears over not seeing my grandchildren.

I never imagined what it would be like to see your grandchildren—to look in their eyes and feel so much love. It's very similar to when you have your own kids. Seeing my daughter and son become parents overwhelmed me emotionally, and those were some of the happiest and most surreal moments of my life.

I've included this chapter to share my experience. I know there are not many lessons here, because I am still learning them. I'll let you know what I find out.

I have to learn to take care of myself and not be offended or hurt by the things that our adult children do that are not what we would do. The way that they feed them, or the things they do with them, we don't have to agree with, because they're not our children. But our hearts hurt, and we worry about our grandchildren just like they're our own children. The big difference between being a mom and Yaya is that we can't do anything about it, because the parents' control everything and have to do what they think is best for their own kids.

I suppose some grandmothers like the fact that they can do all the fun stuff with the grandkids and don't have to worry about the hard parts like teaching them, at least not as much. Most are fond of saying how nice it is to get to be with their grandchildren, to spoil them, and then send them home. I love those things too, but I also take great responsibility to be a great role model for them all. I want to be a woman they look up to are proud of what I did over my lifetime and the wisdom I can share with them and help them through their lives.

Know that your children's grandmothers love your kids so much. They wish sometimes that they could still be your mother, the way they were when you were little and safe in their home. When your mom is crying because she doesn't see you enough, have some grace. You do have to live your life, and we understand that, but be gentle with us grandmothers, because we're going through something, especially those of us who are new at it!

Chapter 13

In the End, it's All About Jesus

"Christianity was never about what you know;
it has always been about Who you know. We know
a lot of What nowadays, but not a lot of Who."
–D. R. Silva

I have been trying to share what I've learned the hard way about being a human, a mom, a daughter, and an image-bearer of God. But I want to finish by saying that in the end, it's all about Jesus. My life changed radically when I gave my life to Christ. If there is one fundamental difference between my mother and me, it is this one thing. Sure, there are lots of differences, but they all spring from one source: I am a Christian. I love and follow Jesus.

I had always had some sort of belief in God. Our family went to church on Christmas and Easter and would have said there was a God and Jesus was real. But when I was around twenty-nine years old, some friends invited Joe and me to a wonderful church, Family Bible, and that's where we stayed.

We grew there, and we raised our kids there. At Family Bible Church, now called Lake Haven, they preach the Gospel, welcome the Holy Spirit, and we would not be where we are today without that fellowship.

There have been so many ups and downs, twists and turns in my life, but only one constant: Jesus. God has always carried us through, even though, sadly, I tend to start down each path I go on without him, thinking that I've got it, that I can do it on my own. I forget and run ahead until I realize that it's not going so well. That's when I remember I not only didn't bring him along, but I never asked him if it was the right path in the first place.

I start each day with him, and I am always working to build better and better morning routines to get the most out of my time with him. Then I can start the day with a foundation. I say that out loud so every cell in my body can hear it. "This is the day that the Lord has made. It's his, I'm his, and he is in control."

I want to be Jesus with skin on. I want the words out of my mouth to be pleasing to him.

I have talked a lot already about purpose, but another aspect of our purpose in this life is to show his love to everyone around us; to show his kindness to others. With the way our world is right now, there has never been a better time than right now to be the hands and feet of Jesus. Showing love, forgiveness, patience, and a capacity to bear with others. Unfortunately, these are not what makes the world go around these days.

I don't have to agree with everything everyone says. I don't have to agree with who people are or what they stand for. I don't have to identify with who they identify with in politics and media, and I don't have to pick a hard side left or right. I will take a hard stance on my character, however, and I won't let anyone or anything change that. Sadly, there have been times in my life when I allowed someone else to change who Sabrina was. I don't do that anymore, because I know who Sabrina is, and so does God. Jesus lives in me, and I am here to be a reflection of him. Will I still make mistakes? I most definitely will. Will I be perfect? No, I will not.

I will ask God to help me to be aware of my mistakes. I want to repair any damage from words that come out of my mouth. I want to show love by giving encouragement and motivation to those who so desperately need it, and I need God to help me.

Jesus to Your Kids

The most difficult people to act like Jesus toward are your own kids. At least that's how it is for me. I once heard somebody at work say, "You know, raising kids is easy."

I thought, "Well, then you're not doing it right."

Raising them well is not easy at all. Your kids mimic everything you do, and you have to be a role model for them all the time. It's a lot of pressure and the stakes are high. Make every moment that you can a learning experience to shape them and grow them, developing them to be strong individuals who can be proud of who they are, but more importantly they can be proud of who God is. Being a parent is a powerful job; maybe the most powerful job there is because of the impact of our children's lives on so many others. The most important thing you can do is teach them how to go to the God who loves them even more than their mama.

The other most important thing you can do as a mom is to go to the Bible for encouragement. Also, read motivational books by Christian authors along with fellowshipping with friends and mentors who have walked through where you are and offer insight.

Is mother the only role women have? Of course not, but it's a key role. How many things are we called to do that men cannot do? Think about it. You may feel called to business, like I am. You may be passionate about something you want to give your time and attention to, such as I do with health, having been a nurse, and now the owner of a wellness company. Guys can do those things, but what they can't do is give birth and offer themselves as a loving mother to little humans; little image-bearers of God who are the next generations. It is God who has given us this privilege and honor, and it is God in Christ who will help us accomplish our role as mothers.

How did I not just grow up and make all the very same mistakes that my own mother did? One thing, or should I say, one person: Jesus. My relationship with him, my surrender to his ways, and his will are the only difference. I love my mother, and when she was a great mom, she was a great mom, but without Jesus in her life, her emptiness drove her again and again to seek fulfillment in romance and new relationships. She is spiritually bankrupt.

What about you? Do you love Jesus more than you love your kids? Do you love him so much that you won't idolize motherhood? Do you accept his love and grace over you on your bad days so that you don't let Satan beat you up and make a bad day worse? I pray that you do. Tell him right now you need his help. Tell him you want to do it with him, his way. Ask him for the grace and the strength to do it.

I would be nowhere without Jesus. Maybe you don't feel the same way, but if you are trying to do this motherhood thing without him, it's going to be a hard road. If you think it's fine, imagine how much better it could be with him. If you know it's not fine, turn to him. You were not made to do it alone.

I love my mom! I got a lot of great things from her, and I respect her. There were lots of years that I couldn't say that, but because of my relationship with God, I respect her out of the character of who I am. I have learned and I'm still learning how I can love and respect her and not take personally the way she lives her life as though she has something against me. Even though she's not the mother that I had thought that I wanted or thought that I deserved, she's the mother I have.

She still is very important to my life, and I would be there for her in an instant. I will support her, defend her, and protect her if I need to. You know, if she got called to the hospital right now, I would drop everything and go there and be there for her. She is my mother, and maybe all the rest of the days of our lives I might shake my head at what she does. And for most of what she does, I do. And it always comes back to this . . .

If it's not one thing, it's a mother.

Chapter 14

Final Thoughts and Some Encouragement

"Being a mother is not about what you gave up to
have a child, but what you gained from having one."
–Sunny Gupta

I LOVE THERAPY. I think everybody can benefit from therapy off and on throughout their life. It's just nice to talk to someone that you can say anything you want to, and a good therapist will give you helpful feedback. The best therapy I've had was in group therapy environments and intensives. There's nothing like setting aside a whole three-day period so that all day, every day you can relentlessly get at what needsto be gotten at!

We've been to all kinds of therapy and personal growth workshops. I'm committed to growing, and I don't think it happens very well without intentionality. We go out of town to seminars for marriage, business, healing, and really any kind of personal development.

I'll admit I'm addicted to personal growth. I've always loved just digging, digging, and digging deeper. We attended Tony Robbins's Unleash the Power Within event, and we've done the business mastery workshops. We've gone through Dave Ramsey's Financial Peace University, and we just love working on ourselves.

You know, I believe if you're not progressing, then you're stagnating and dying. I have arrived at a place now where I'm content, accepting, and happy with who I am in my life, but I still want to always look for ways to live better and live happier. If you'll commit to growing, then you will grow. I don't mean to consume knowledge and make no changes, but to try things. Learn and put into practice what seems like it's going to enrich your life. I know there are self-help junkies who live with the illusion that they are growing because they are consuming knowledge, but you have to put at least some of it into practice. I truly pray that you put into practice some of what I've said in this book.

Whether you find yourself mothering your mother, mothering your children, or mothering your pets, friends, neighbors, or nieces, "mother" is a powerful identity. There's a lot of pressure that comes with motherhood because people look up to and take wisdom from that mother in their life.

Everybody's looking for the mother, the matriarch, to have it all figured out. They listen with open ears. What's mom going to say? There's a lot of pressure to get it right. That's the message of this whole book. There's a lot of pressure, so go to God. Walk in love and get that love from him. You can't go wrong if you stay committed.

My hope and prayer for you is that even if, like me, you go through hard and heavy times on your motherhood journey, you will close this book and feel, like me by the grace of God, lighthearted and hopeful. I hope you will choose hope, love, and the lightheartedness every day that comes from truly casting your burdens onto the God who can bear them. He says, "Live carefree before God; he is most careful with you" (1 Pt 5:7).

You really can let the burdens go. Don't be addicted to your burdens, but give them to God, and then just stand strong walking through motherhood and abide in him all the rest of your days.

Today, as I write the last sentences of this book, I love my mom. I respect her and I'll be there for her and protect her every way I can, but I have learned the lessons of continual boundaries to protect Sabrina at the same time.

I choose to focus on the things that I love and to realize that Mom may never live out the life I wish for her because it's HER life, but I can still pray for her true happiness.

We had the opportunity to celebrate her birthday last weekend, and as I type this I shake my head and think about all the things she did and said, and there may be another book on the horizon if she doesn't settle down.

Oh well. IF IT'S NOT ONE THING IT'S A MOTHER. God bless you!

ABOUT THE AUTHOR

Sabrina is a self-confessed go-getter!

With a driving ambition as strong as her desire to help people feel and be their absolute best inside and out, she fulfilled a lifelong dream by opening the evolutionary wellness center in West Palm Beach 'Immunity Health.'

Refreshingly honest and aware of her strengths and weaknesses, Sabrina nurtured her natural impulse to inspire hope, health, and resilience in others through her own life experience as a nurse, certified fitness instructor, magazine publisher, author, and extremely proud mom. Outside of her illustrious career and unstoppable determination to achieve, you'll find Sabrina and her devoted, hard-working husband, Joe, enjoying time with their large family. Having lovingly fostered and adopted many children over the years, It's no surprise they were named the 2014 Foster Parents of the Year by Kids Central Inc.

In a perfect world, everyone would take care of themselves, but when they can't, Sabrina will!

www.ingramcontent.com/pod-product-compliance
Lightning Source LLC
Chambersburg PA
CBHW071750150726
47998CB00005B/1885